MORAL REVOLUTION
Let's talk about it: SEXUALITY

Welcome to the REVOLUTION!

In a world where our students are surrounded by the new "normals" of hooking-up, sexting, homosexuality, abortion, and high-speed porn addiction, it is more important than ever to educate, equip and empower our young people with practical truth and wisdom in their battle for purity. There is a sexual revolution emerging, in both religious and secular environments, to break free from the effects of addictions, depression, broken families and relationships, which are all too common in our society. We believe that healthy people are prone to make healthy sexual choices. And healthy sexual choices result in freedom!

In your hands is a countercultural sexual education course that transforms how our children view sexuality through intelligent and unbiased education, providing real solutions to core issues surrounding our sexuality. Sex is not love. Intimacy does not just happen between the sheets. Sex is not just a physical encounter. Purity is not just abstinence. Sexual education is not just a biological or theological issue. It is a multidimensional issue that requires a holistic perspective and approach.

This course combines biblical truth, scientific understanding and tools to provide you with a well-rounded, interactive, multimedia experience. This will enable you to teach your students well. We believe that as a result, your students will walk in greater health and freedom. Our goal is that that they take what they have learned in this course from the classroom and into their bedrooms, relationships and households.

It is time to demystify sex. It is time to bring it into the light of purity, hope and unconditional love. It is time to take the power of sexuality out of the enemy's hands and place it back where it rightly belongs: in the hands of the children of the living God. Make no mistake, it is not an accident that you are in the trenches, teaching, equipping and training His people right now. For such a time as this! Thank you for positioning yourself for His service in this generation. May God bless you with His anointing, wisdom and grace as you lead, teach and empower. And know this— you are not alone.

You are part of the Revolution!

Cover Design & Layout by Hans Bennewitz

Special Thanks to the amazing 2013-2014 interns of Moral Revolution. Cara Santos, Soo Prince, Jonathan Patrick, Jessica Kopp, Ale Seikmeier and Anna Weygandt, we could not have done this without you!

WHAT'S IT ABOUT?

This 6-week course is all about sexuality! We cover who God is; the nature of the One who created us, our bodies, sex etc. We look at how to shift our view and identity in order to align our view with His. We then cover our physical, emotional and spiritual makeup and how each part interlinks and interacts. We talk about what is going on in our bodies when we have sex, what our needs are, and how to steward them well. Lastly we cover restoration and covenant. God is always wanting to restore, redeem and make new, no matter how many times we fail. However, we want to get really good at managing ourselves well so that we can live free from shame and cyclical behaviour.

WHO'S IT FOR?

- Youth Pastors/Leaders
- Teenagers
- Parents
- Small Group Leaders
- Young Adults
- College Pastors

WHAT DO I GET?

Six 'ready to teach' lessons covering the subject of sexuality.
Each lesson contains the following:

- A Teacher's Guide to brief you on the principles of a particular lesson
- A 'Learn It' section—a complete lesson plan including illustrations and media clips
- A 'Lead It' section—ideas for how to close the session and lead a ministry time
- Reflection and Activation Opportunities
- Ideas for props
- Lots of scripture
- Resources such as: the Purity Plan and Purity Covenant

HOW DO I USE IT?

This course was created to enable you as a teacher to teach on sexuality without having to do all the work of pulling the material together. Having said that, we would strongly encourage you, as the teacher, to read through the entire course material first. Familiarize yourself with it, look up the links (particularly those related to the scientific material) to really get under the skin of the content and own it as your own!

We offer various options for illustrations and props for each lesson, so choose what you feel is appropriate for your students; you know them best! If possible, include your own anecdotes or stories to personalise the series.

The lessons all contain a multitude of scriptures, the idea isn't that you necessarily use them all! Pick the ones you feel will 'flow' with your ownership of the lesson.

Each lesson is designed to take you about 45 minutes, though you can adjust it to fit the size and needs of your group. You may also want to have Participant Guides available, which contain personal reflective questions for individual students to work through or can be used in a small group setting.

FINAL THOUGHTS

Our aim is to provide resources to assist you in equipping your students. We understand that with the vastness of this subject it's impossible to completely cover everything on the topic. We also understand that it's a very sensitive and unique topic. With that said, we would appeal to you to please be aware of the tone in which you communicate. We are an anti-shame movement and purpose to lead in this way. We ask that you approach this course with caution, humility, grace and unconditional love, just as the Father leads us!

We pray that God gives you wisdom on how to best utilize this material to fully educate and empower your students.

God bless you!

TABLE OF CONTENTS

SIX-WEEK SUMMARY

Lesson 1: SEX+GOD

How we learned about sex will largely dictate what we believe about sex. In this lesson, we discuss three possible environments that taught us what to believe about sex and what message they taught us. We will then tackle three common lies we may believe about the nature of God by discovering the truth that represents Him in scripture. Through these exercises, we discover that God is not angry, distant, or indifferent, but is an approachable, caring Father who wants to be present to teach His children how to manage their sexuality well.

Lesson 2: SEX+IDENTITY

We must understand the way God, the Creator of sex, understands sex, so we can view it rightly. God has a big 'YES' regarding sex and a protective 'NO' in place for our success. Father God has given us powerful sex drives on purpose! But, with great power, comes great responsibility. In this lesson, we discuss that God gives us the ability to make choices for ourselves in order that we might experience freedom and relationship with Him. Because our choices are the outward appearance of our inward beliefs, we also discuss five foundational truths that help us further understand God's nature and strengthen our identity as His children, resulting in us making healthy, powerful choices.

Lesson 3: SEX+THE BODY—Part 1

This first half of a two-part lesson finally dives into the dynamic effects of sex on our physical bodies, as well as the emotional realm of our souls. This countercultural sex-talk proves that sex is not merely a physical encounter, but an all-encompassing act that was created by God not only to make babies or for pleasure, but for us to experience deep, multidimensional union with another human being. In his lesson, we scientifically discuss that at the point of arousal, a hormonal chain-reaction begins within our brains and bodies, which is meant to lead us from arousal to climax, motivating us toward sex by various levels of chemical (hormonal) reward. In light of this, we investigate where and how to draw sexual boundary lines for ourselves by understanding our own bodies and what we are aroused by. (Note: While the language in this lesson is used scientifically, it is more explicit than previous lessons. We will be defining sex (vaginal, anal, oral), arousal, and orgasm, though these are not the focal points of the lesson.)

Lesson 4: SEX+THE BODY—Part 2

In the concluding lesson of SEX+THE BODY, we learn that each part of our being (spirit, soul, body) has specific needs that must be met for us to thrive spiritually, emotionally, and physically. In this lesson, we focus on the needs of our spirits and souls, because, "when we get our soul and spirit needs met, our physical needs quiet down," and our sex drives become manageable. We discuss what our needs are and what sources we should go to in order to get them filled. We also discuss that abusing these sources or using them inappropriately has negative outcomes, which may include sexually inappropriate and unhealthy, addictive behaviors. The basic principle is this: when we do not get our spiritual needs met by God, first and foremost, our bodies and emotions begin to rule our lives as we subconsciously compensate for the lack in our souls and spirits. A spirit-led person is a healthy, pure person!

Lesson 5: SEX + RESTORATION

We have all made decisions that we wish we hadn't. And all too often, we let regret, shame, and fear be the loudest voice in our lives, especially when it comes to our sexuality. In this lesson, we take an honest look at the effects sexual sin has on us and why, but we don't stop there! In our discussion, we look at the great hope and plan God has for restoration in each part of our being—spirit, soul and body. Though sexual sin has consequences in each of these realms of our being, Jesus' sacrifice and forgiveness makes full restoration available to those who turn to Him in repentance. There is a fresh start available for every part of everyone. This includes the healing of our connection with Him, our emotions, our memories, and even our physical bodies, making us like new! (Note: In this lesson, we talk about soul-ties, a connection formed between people, especially through sexual relationships. These can be both healthy and beneficial and unhealthy and destructive. This lesson also emphasizes the topic of premarital sex.)

Lesson 6: SEX + COVENANT

Our focus in lesson six? Covenant, self-awareness, accountability, community, vision. Our last session will be spent setting vision for a life of holiness and getting tools to help us practically walk in (sexual) purity! We are not asking our teens to "kiss dating goodbye" or to take a vow of chastity for life, but instead, are asking them to learn themselves and begin to manage getting their needs met in a healthy way; remember, we often make poor sexual choices because we are trying to meet our needs in inappropriate, ineffective, or unhealthy ways. With that in mind, we start our conversation with the understanding that we absolutely need God's grace as well as His ability, resources, and support to be pure. We can do nothing without Him but we can do all things through His strength! We will invite the students to begin to walk in covenant with God. This will mean saying 'YES' to some things and 'NO' to others; this is how to build a pure life! We will finish our series by creating individual purity plans which will act as roadmaps to lead us in success to our goals for purity, wholeness, and sex!

01 LESSON ONE SEX + GOD

TEACHING GUIDE

This lesson introduces the idea that we need to understand the true character of the God who invented sex, before we can fully understand the sex He meant for us to experience.

There are many lies we may believe about God. These are ideas that have been told to us, preached at us, or ones we have concluded from our personal observations of life. These lies don't line up with God's true character and nature as revealed in scripture. In order for us to truly live out a healthy sexuality, we must unpack these belief systems and expose them for what they are: lies.

In the beginning of this study, you will help the listeners identify some of the constructs or environments that have shaped their belief systems, knowledge, and perspectives on sex. In order to do this, we have outlined three different environments in which they may have learned about sex. Our goal is to break them down in order to make sense of the reasons behind their perspectives on sex. Our hope is to help listeners identify the lens through which

 OBJECTIVES

1. How You Learned About Sex
2. God Created Sex
3. Character of God

 SCRIPTURES

Romans 8:31–39 (MSG)
Psalm 139:7–12 (NLT)
Numbers 14:18 (NIV)
Psalm 84:11 (NLT)
Jeremiah 29:11 (VOICE)

 SUPPLIES (OPTIONAL)

- Door
- Bucket
- Poster Board
- Red Marker
- iPhone/Newspaper
- Whole Baked Pie, Spoon, Napkin or Plate

they filter their information and discover new ways to embrace a healthy perspective—God's perspective—on sex.

First, we have the **silent** environment. In this environment, we learn sex is neither good nor bad; it is simply never talked about. However, in the absence of opinion, the message is still clear: sex is unimportant. Whether due to fear, ignorance, or standards of privacy, no time is given to teaching the value of sex and its inherent nature. We are to explore this topic on our own and form our own conclusions. From this environment, an easy conclusion would be: "If the most important people in my life don't place any value or importance on sex, then why should I?"

Second, we have the **saturated** environment. This environment is very vocal about sex. It is expressed and exposed in the form of jokes, movies, media and casual relationships. Its crude and disrespectful nature communicates the opposite of sex's true significance and purpose. This environment exploits sex, paying no attention to its sacredness. As a result, no regard is held for the body-soul-spirit connection taking place. From this environment, an easy conclusion would be: "Sex is nothing more than a physical act, and anything else experienced is over-thinking a simple encounter."

Thirdly, we have the **conflicted** environment. This environment is sending mixed signals about sex, communicating both value and shame. Though intentions are good, the result is a fear-based audience making decisions without understanding or purpose. This can be just as harmful as the previous two environments, because without a personal connection to the "why," our desire to have sex often trumps "the rules" we follow. We know enough to aim for purity, but not always enough to maintain it. From this environment, an easy conclusion would be: "I'm just going to try to do what's right because it's right, and hopefully I don't blow it."

Regardless of the environment each of the students have learned from, we have a greater teacher, the "Holy Spirit" who will help you lead and teach on this subject. More than your desire, God's desire is that each man and woman would know and have confidence about this sacred and honorable subject. We believe you can teach this simply because you are saying, "Here I am Lord, send me." Now buckle up and hold on, because you're about to begin an incredible journey into this vast subject called SEX.

Welcome/Introduction *(10 minutes)*

Our goal today is to simply start a conversation with you about sex. It's not just to give you facts or Bible verses, but also to help you understand the whole picture of what God intended for sex when He created it. This may surprise you, but God started this conversation many years ago and has a lot to say on the topic. Before we get into what He has to say, we want to help you understand the different types of environments you may have been raised in and how sex may have been communicated to you. As we talk about the three types of environment, see if you can identify the one you were raised in.

Whether we knew it or not, most of us were raised in an environment that communicated strongly about sex. These environments have created the filters through which we view and approach sex today.

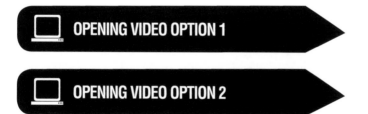

OPENING VIDEO OPTION 1

Sex — Moral Revolution

Video Description:
Guys and girls share their thoughts on sex within marriage and outside of marriage.

OPENING VIDEO OPTION 2

Dad Sex Talk — *What Women Want*

Video Description:
As his daughter's prom approaches, Nick decides to have a talk with her about sex.

1. SILENT ENVIRONMENT

- We learned sex was neither good nor bad, just never talked about.

- The message was—sex is a part of life, but unimportant and too private to talk about.

- Time was not given to explain the value of sex.

- We were left to discover and to learn about sex on our own.

 ILLUSTRATION OPTION 1

iPhone Analogy: Bring your lesson to life! Use your iPhone's mute button for the "Silent Environment," where talking about sex is so quiet, you never hear it. You can either show an image of it or act it out by mouthing a sentence or two.

 ILLUSTRATION OPTION 2

Door Analogy: Use a door to illustrate how sex was a "closed" topic. Shut and lock a door, showing there was no access to the sexual information or experiences inside that "room."

- Does this sound familiar to you? "If the most important people in my life don't place any value or importance on sex, then why should I?"

- God is not silent about sex, and we want to explore the topic with you today.

2. SATURATED ENVIRONMENT

- We learned what sex is through crude jokes, explicit movies, and casual sexual relationships.

- Sex is strictly physical; no communication about the body, soul, spirit, connection.

- We don't feel there's much to learn about sex (the physical act), because we have heard and seen every detail of it through movies, music, books, and experiences.

⊙ ILLUSTRATION OPTION 1

iPhone Analogy: Bring your lesson to life! Use the speakerphone function for the "Saturated Environment," where talk about sex is so loud, you can always hear it. You can either use an image on the screen or talk louder than normal.

⊙ ILLUSTRATION OPTION 2

Door Analogy: Use a door to illustrate how sex was an "open" topic. Remove the door from the frame, or, alternatively, prop it open so it cannot shut, showing that there was no way to avoid seeing the sexual information or experiences inside that "room."

- Does this sound familiar to you? "It's okay to view sex as being nothing more than a physical experience; anything more is over-thinking a simple encounter."

- God created sex to be more than physical.

3. CONFLICTED ENVIRONMENT

- We learn about the value and the sacredness of sex, while also being told that sex is shameful and disgusting when handled inappropriately.

- The message is that any sexual desire before marriage is shameful and to be avoided, yet, euphoric, something to be enjoyed after marriage.

- We end up being scared into purity, denying our sexual desire, or hiding in shame when we act on that desire.

> **⊙ ILLUSTRATION OPTION 1**
>
> **iPhone Analogy:** Bring your lesson to life! For the "Conflicted Environment," act out a 3-way call, where the audience doesn't know what to think, because they're hearing two opposing opinions on a subject.

> **⊙ ILLUSTRATION OPTION 1**
>
> **Door Analogy:** Use a door to illustrate how sex was a "back-and-forth" topic. Allow the door to swing back and forth between its open and closed position, showing that there was no defined or predictable access to sexual information and experiences; the door could swing open or shut in your face at any moment.

- Does this sound familiar? "I'm just going to try to do what's right because it's right, and hopefully I don't blow it."

- God meant for our sexual desires to be met in a healthy way throughout our whole lives.

Our goal throughout this series is to give you a clear message about sex. We will be as honest as possible. We will give you facts about what God intended for sex, and help you understand the different needs you have as men and women. We will also reveal God's wild love for you. We will view our past as He does— as 100% redeemable.

Whether you are hearing this topic for the first time or you have already been sexual active, we will all learn something new. But first, you've got to know: God loves you, His heart is for you, and He is incredibly passionate about SEX because He invented it!

Now we are going to look at the character of God. It's impossible to trust someone's opinion without understanding their motives.

Let's take a few minutes and look at the lies we can easily believe about God.

 **Learn It** *(30 minutes)*

1. LIE #1—GOD **CAN REJECT** YOU.

DEFINE IT: "Reject" dismissed as failing

The Idea: God won't answer your call. He refuses to have relationship with you because you're not perfect.

Truth: The nature of God is unconditional love. He's for you. He can't help but love you and want you to succeed. God *is* love; He'd have to reject Himself to reject you.

- **God's Nature is Unconditional.**
  Romans 8:31–39 (MSG) So, what do you think? With God on our side like this, how can we lose? If God didn't hesitate to put everything on the line for us, embracing our condition

and exposing himself to the worst by sending his own Son, is there anything else he wouldn't gladly and freely do for us? And who would dare tangle with God by messing with one of God's chosen? Who would dare even to point a finger? The One who died for us—who was raised to life for us!—is in the presence of God at this very moment sticking up for us. Do you think anyone is going to be able to drive a wedge between us and Christ's love for us? There is no way! Not trouble, not hard times, not hatred, not hunger, not homelessness, not bullying threats, not backstabbing, not even the worst sins listed in Scripture: They kill us in cold blood because they hate you. We're sitting ducks; they pick us off one by one. None of this fazes us because Jesus loves us. I'm absolutely convinced that nothing—nothing living or dead, angelic or demonic, today or tomorrow, high or low, thinkable or unthinkable—absolutely nothing can get between us and God's love because of the way that Jesus our Master has embraced us.

⊙ ILLUSTRATION OPTION 1

iPhone Analogy: Act out "God not taking a call." Use the decline button on your iPhone or show an image of the decline button when you dial Him, or alternatively, when someone calls you.

⊙ ILLUSTRATION OPTION 2

Big X: Using a red marker, draw a big "X" on poster board, and hold it up when someone tries to interact with you, or when you try to interact with "God."

2. LIE #2—WHEN HE IS HURT OR ANGRY, GOD **CAN IGNORE** YOU

The Idea: God disconnects from you when He doesn't want to hear you or deal with your problems.

Truth: You can't surprise God. He does not disconnect from you. God is not afraid of your sin. He doesn't run from it; He runs into it. He is not impulsive. He is always present.

- **God Doesn't Disconnect**
  Psalm 139:7–12 (NLT) "I can never escape from your spirit! I can never get away from your presence! If I go up to heaven, you are there; if I go down to the place of the dead, you are there. If I ride the wings of the morning, if I dwell by the farthest oceans, even there your hand will guide me, and your strength will support me. I could ask the darkness to hide me and the light around me to become night — but even in darkness I cannot hide from you. To you the night shines as bright as day. Darkness and light are both alike to you."

- **God Is Not Impulsive**
  Numbers 14:18 (NIV) "The Lord is slow to anger, abounding in love and forgiving sin and rebellion."

◉ ILLUSTRATION OPTION 1

iPhone Analogy: Act out "God muting a call." Use the mute button on your iPhone or show an image of the mute button when He answers your call, or alternatively, when someone calls you.

◉ ILLUSTRATION OPTION 2

Newspaper Analogy: Flip open a newspaper and hold it in front of your face to show God ignoring the audience or individual in front of Him.

3. LIE #3—GOD **CAN WITHHOLD** FROM YOU

The Idea: God has good things for you, but He's holding out on you. He is controlling and stingy. He doesn't give you full access to the fun or enjoyable things He has given you. Because we believe this lie, we go out and get what we need in other places outside of Him.

Truth – He loves YOU! He is FOR YOU! God can withhold FOR you, but not FROM you. God doesn't punish you by withholding Himself from you.

- **God Only Gives His Best**

  Jeremiah 29:11 (VOICE) "For I know the plans I have for you," says the Eternal, "plans for peace, not evil, to give you a future and hope—never forget that."

  Psalm 84:11 (NLT) "For the Lord God is our sun and our shield. He gives us grace and glory. The Lord will withhold no good thing from those who do what is right."

> **◉ ILLUSTRATION OPTION 1**
>
> **iPhone Analogy:** Use your iPhone to act out a parent setting strict parental controls on the phone being given to their son/daughter. Alternatively, show an image of the parental control settings. Act out the frustration of not being able to use all the apps, or, for example, having the phone turn off at a certain time.

> **⊙ ILLUSTRATION OPTION 2**
>
> **Whole Baked Pie:** Use a pie, spoon, and plate or napkin. Pretend you're giving away the whole pie. Then change your mind and serve a portion of pie onto a plate or napkin. At first, only serve a tiny portion—a small bite or two, or only the crust. Then serve a sloppy, ugly serving, by scooping out another portion with a spoon or, for effect, your bare hand, and slap it onto the plate carelessly. Offer it to someone.

- *The idea*: God has good things for you, but He's holding out on you. He is controlling and stingy. He doesn't give you full access to the fun or enjoyable things He has given you. Because we believe this lie, we go out and get what we need in other places outside of Him.

Love It *(15 minutes)**

REFLECTION TIME *(Personal)*

1. How did you first learn about sex and what was your first thought?

2. When you have questions about sex, where do you go for answers?

3. Have you ever felt like you couldn't talk to God about what's going on inside of you? Why?

CONNECTION QUESTIONS *(Small Group)*

1. Out of the three environments (silent, saturated, conflicted) which one sounds most familiar, and why?

2. Out of the three main lies about God (God can reject me, God can ignore me, God can withhold from me) which did you most identify with, and why?

3. What one thing most surprised you about God, and why?

4. Q&A (Take time to help answer any additional questions they may have)

 **Live It** *(15 minutes)* **

Homework

1. MY LIFE—Take a moment this week to talk to God about sex. Tell Him what you think about it—everything! For example— what you know, what you're ashamed of, what you like about it. Then write down anything you think God says to you. *It's okay if you don't hear anything right away!*

2. MY FRIENDS—When your friends start talking about sex, pay attention to how they talk about it and how it makes you feel.

3. MY WORLD—Have you ever noticed how much sex sells? Begin to look for this in music, movies, and advertisements.

★ Lead It (5 minutes)

As the leader, choose to end your session in a way that suits the needs, dynamics, and vision of your group. The goal is to build trust and encourage vulnerability, both within the group and between individuals and God. You know your group best; choose the option that fits you!

1. CLOSING WITHOUT MINISTRY

- Explain the journey of the next five weeks
- Encourage them to let God redefine everything they think they know/believe about sex, love, and virginity.

2. SMALL GROUPS CLOSING

- Have them break up into groups of 3–5 people
- Use Reflection/Connection Points above

3. MINISTRY TIME CLOSING

- Explain that some of them have never talked to God about their sexual desire, and encourage them to take a moment to start the conversation with Him.
- Have them ask God if they have believed one of the lies that we've talked about today. Pray over them, asking God to reveal the truth to them.

* Optional small group time.

** Optional homework or encounter time for the student to do on his/her own.

02 LESSON TWO SEX + IDENTITY

TEACHING GUIDE

This lesson introduces the truth that, from the beginning of creation, God has been saying YES to our dreams, our desires and even our sex drives. Like any great thing, knowing the "rules of engagement" enables us to have the best time to get the fullest experience. Roller coasters are a great example of this—they are incredibly fun, exciting, and keep our adrenaline on high; yet without the proper information given, we may not have a good experience with them. For instance, if no one told us to leave our hats, phones, and personal items on the side, then we may lose something of value. If the ride operator never tells us to keep our hands and legs in the cart before and during the ride, we could be severely injured. Or worse, if the designer didn't think to put seat belts and handle bars on the roller coaster, we would have all died on our first time through. No one is saying 'NO' to roller coasters but they are saying YES, with boundaries.

The same goes for God. He is a good Father! He created good things for us. He is not asking us to put up "CLOSED: Please Come Back

OBJECTIVES

1. God Has a Yes
2. You Are a Powerful Person
3. With Power Comes Responsibility

SCRIPTURES

Gen 2:15–17 (NIV)
Jeremiah 29:11(NIV)
1 Corinthians 6:16–20 (MSG)

SUPPLIES (OPTIONAL)

- Large poster board
- Sharpie
- 6 pieces of 8.5 x 11 paper

Later" signs over our sexuality; He is saying YES to it, with boundaries. The focus of God saying "NO" to us having sex before marriage is the wrong focus. We need to turn our heads to see Him shouting YES to us having the absolute best and safest experience of sex. Like every other area of our lives, when we say YES to one thing, we are inevitably saying NO to something else.

In order to live out this reality, particularly in the area of sex, the right belief systems about God and ourselves are required. In this lesson, we take the students through five powerful beliefs that will help empower them to strongly start off their journey to purity and manage their sex drives with strength and longevity. Taking time to ground ourselves in these truths will help shape our lives and prepare us for whatever may come, including, but not limited to, our sex lives.

The following are the '5 Power Beliefs' that we must be able to claim for ourselves before we can embrace this journey of taking full responsibility for our lives—and our sex drives.

First, I believe God is who He says He is and that He does what He says He'll do. God wants us to have it all—a full life, healthy relationships, a fruitful marriage, and a fulfilling sex life. He created sex between a man and a woman, and everything He creates is good*. *(See Gen 1:28; 1 Tim 4:4)

Second, I believe God can be trusted because He is consistent and always gives me His best. God is not looking at my life linearly; He sees the whole picture. Therefore, I trust His perspective and advice for my life because, He sees and understands things that I have yet to experience or comprehend.

Third, I believe, with God's help, there is nothing I can't do. God's Spirit gives us the ability and the power to manage our lives in any given situation. Therefore, regardless of person or circumstance, I am responsible at all times for controlling my decisions and responses, and for keeping love as my first priority.

Fourth, I believe that every person, including myself, is due and worthy of honor. I will honor you, not because of your titles or choices, but because I am honorable. Furthermore, I choose to honor myself and my body by protecting what has been entrusted to me by a loving Father.

Fifth, I believe my story is worth telling! God writes great stories full of redemption and adventure, and I must believe He is excited to write mine as well. Because He uniquely created me with intention, detail, and purpose, the role I play in His grand production is irreplaceable.

This week is all about creating foundational beliefs that will help each of your students. Don't worry about making it a "sex talk" yet. Focus on laying the right foundation so that when we do talk about sex next week, we have done the prepared the way. We challenge you to take time to ground yourself in these truths too. It will help form you as a leader and protect your heart as well.

Welcome/Introduction *(10 minutes)*

The Bible says, when you believe in the right things, the right things happen. Whether you know it or not God gave you the ability to manage and to take responsibility for your whole life. We will show you five grounding truths that will empower you to do so and hopefully become your greatest tools. God, as your loving Father, desires for you to only have only His best in your life. He doesn't hide what we need, but clearly gives us what we need in order to live out a powerful and healthy life… even in our sex lives. God says YES to our sexuality. In other words, God only says "no" to sex outside of marriage in order to protect us from the consequences of bonding with someone whom we are not in covenant relationship with.

Whether it feels like it or not, we are all capable of controlling the strong desires we have for the opposite sex, but it all begins with what we believe about ourselves. As long as we believe that we are subject to our hormones, our circumstances, or others'

🖥️ OPENING VIDEO OPTION 1

Father Wounds

Video Description:
Kris Vallotton shares about the importance of relating to God as Father, as well as having spiritual Fathers to speak into our lives.

🖥️ OPENING VIDEO OPTION 2

A Good Father—*Big Daddy*

Video Description:
During the custody battle for Julian, Sonny tells the court and his own father, who is prosecuting him, why he would be a good father.

choices, then we will never take ownership for the choices we have made or are making now. The best part about choosing to be powerful is that we have vision and purpose for how we have chosen to live our lives. We are excited about what we have access to, not disappointed or jealous about what we don't, because we understand the heart behind the boundary set up for us.

🖥️ **OPENING VIDEO OPTION 1**

🖥️ **OPENING VIDEO OPTION 2**

🔍 Learn It (30 minutes)

1. GOD HAS A YES!

- God's heart is for us to have it all—our desires, our dreams, a great sex life.

- Because He loves us and we're worth protecting, He only says "no" when we aren't staying within the (protective) boundaries He's set up for us to succeed.

2. GARDEN OF EDEN

- **Everything was YES, but with boundaries**
  Genesis 2:15–17 (MSG): "God took the Man and set him down in the Garden of Eden to work the ground and keep it in order. God commanded the Man, "You can eat from any tree in the garden, except from the Tree-of-Knowledge-of-Good-and-Evil. Don't eat from it. The moment you eat from that tree, you're dead.""

- God gives Adam and Eve the information they need to thrive in the Garden.

- Only after they fail to live within those boundaries does God have to say "no" to the Garden, in order to protect them from eternal separation from Him.

- Giving us a choice made us powerful and free to choose.

 OPENING VIDEO OPTION 3

 **OPENING VIDEO OPTION 3**

***Bruce Almighty –*
Love and Free Will**

Video Description:
When Grace breaks up with Bruce, Bruce wonders to God how he can make someone love him without affecting free will.

(While they are watching the video have someone bring up the white poster board w/ the following 5 Power Beliefs and their declarations written under each of them.)

3. POWER AND RESPONSIBILITY

- Because God gives you a choice it makes you a powerful person!

- But with great power comes great responsibility.

- Your choices come out of what you believe.

- What you believe becomes the most powerful force in your life.

Power Beliefs

1. I BELIEVE GOD

- **God is Truth, it's one of His names**
  John 14:6 (NIV): "I am the way and the truth and the life" *(John uses the Greek word for truth 25 times and links it closely with Jesus, who is the Truth)*

- **God doesn't lie**
  Matt 17:20 (NIV): "I tell you the truth, if you have faith as small as a mustard seed, you can say to this Mountain, "Move" *(31 times in*

Matthew (NIV) Jesus says "I tell you the truth"); *Numbers 23:19 (NIV):* "God is not a man, that he should lie, nor a son of man, that he should change his mind. Does he speak and then not act? Does he promise and not fulfill?") *(see also Heb. 6:18)*

- **He is who He says He is**
  Exodus 3:14 (NIV): "I Am Who I Am… I Am has sent me…"; *1 Cor 1:9* (NLT) "God will do this, for he is faithful to do what He says, and he has invited you into partnership with His Son, Jesus Christ our Lord" *(see also Rev 1:8 (NLT); Rev 1:17b–18)*

- **He does what He says He is going to do**
  Isa 43:16 (NIV): "I am the Lord, who opened a way through the waters, making a dry path through the sea"; Rev 3:7–8 (NIV) "What he opens no-one can shut, and what he shuts no-one can open….See, I have placed before you an open door that no-one can shut"

2. I TRUST GOD

- **He is trustworthy**
  Isa 49:23b (NLT): "I am the Lord. Those who trust in me will never be put to shame" *(see also 2 Sam 7:28, Deut. 32:4)*

- **He is always the same**
  Heb 13:8 (NIV): "Jesus Christ is the same yesterday and today and forever"

- **He is all knowing & understanding**
  Psalm 139:3 (NIV): "You discern my going out and my lying down; you are familiar with all my ways" *(see also Isa 55:9)*

- **He will always give us His best**
  Rom 8:32 (NIV): "He who did not spare his own Son, but gave Him up for us all—how will He not also, along with Him, graciously give us all things" *(see also Psalm 84:11, Jer 29:11, Rom 8:28)*

- **He will never leave me**
  Deut 31:8 (NIV): "The Lord himself goes before you and will be with you; He will never leave you or forsake you. Do not be afraid; do not be discouraged" *(see also Isa 42:16, Rom 8:37, Isa 41:10, Isa 43:13)*

3. I AM POWERFUL

- **I can do all things**
  Php 4:13 (NIV): "I can do everything through Him who gives me strength" *(see also Isa 40:31, Isa 41:10, Eph 3:16)*

- **I am responsible for my choices**
  Deut 30:19–20 (NLT): "Today I have given you the choice between life and death, between blessings and curses. Now I call on heaven and earth to witness the choice you make. Oh, that you would choose life, so that you and your descendants might live! You can make this choice by loving the LORD your God, obeying him, and committing yourself firmly to Him. This is the key to your life" *(see also 2 Pet 1:5–7, Gal 5:23, 1 Thess 5:8, Luke 4:14, Acts 1:8)*

- **My past does not define my future**
  Isa 43:25 (VOICE): "So let's get this clear: it's for My own sake that I save you. I am He who wipes the slate clean and erases your wrongdoing. I will not call to mind your sins anymore" *(see also Isa 1:18)*

4. I AM HONORABLE

- **I am valuable**
  1 Cor 6:20 (NIV): "...you were bought at a price. Therefore honor God with your bodies"

- **I honor others**
  Php 2:3 (NIV): "Do nothing out of selfish ambition or vain conceit. Rather, in humility value others above yourselves" *(see also Mark 12:33)*

- **I am called to love at all times**
  Prov 17:17 (VOICE): "A true friend loves regardless of the situation, and a real brother exists to share the tough times"

5. I AM SIGNIFICANT

- **I play a vital role in God's great story**
  Esther 4:14 (NIV): "And who knows but that you have come to your royal position for such a time as this?" *(Esther was pivotal to the saving of her nation. You are being invited into a story of unique significance. Your life is not just about you, but those people that you will impact & influence)*

- **My story is full of redemption and adventure!** *Look at* **Moses, David & Peter.** *They all messed up, had encounters with God and through their restoration and redemption became significant leaders that impacted the masses. You have never messed up 'too much' and it's never too late to re-engage with the adventure!*

- **He sees the end from the beginning**
  Psalm 139:16 (NIV): "...all the days ordained for me were written in your book before one of them came to be" *(see also Rev 22:13)*

- **He has good plans for me**
  Jer 29:11 (NIV) "For I know the plans I have for you" declares the Lord, "plans to prosper you and not to harm you, plans to give you hope and a future"

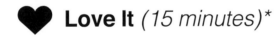 **Love It** *(15 minutes)**

REFLECTION TIME *(Personal)*

DEFINE IT: "Honor" great respect; high esteem

1. Do you view and treat yourself like this? If not, take a moment to ask God what it is that is clouding your vision and preventing you from valuing yourself.

2. When you think about God's boundaries, do you find you want to rebel, argue or submit? Be honest with yourself and Him. Do you believe a lie about what He's like?

3. Are you living in your own small story, thinking just about how your actions affect you, or are you daring to believe that you are called to influence many and that your choices for integrity, (when no-one but God is looking) matter?

CONNECTION QUESTIONS *(small group)*

1. Are you able to say 'yes' to God when He sets a boundary or is it a struggle? Discuss this; be vulnerable to share why, perhaps in some areas you aren't.

2. What does it mean to be powerful and yet to be submitted at the same time? Discuss.

3. Have you 'blown it' recently? Know that Jesus totally sympathizes with your weakness and is full of redemption. Confess to Him, confess to each other, love on each other.

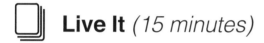 **Live It** *(15 minutes)*

Homework

1. MY LIFE—Take time this week to determine and reflect on these 5 power beliefs.

2. MY FRIENDS—Find a group of trustworthy friends that have similar beliefs and can help hold you accountable to these beliefs.

3. MY WORLD—In your daily life, ask yourself what is currently influencing your beliefs? (e.g. media, church, peers, parents, government, etc.) Have you chosen them for yourself?

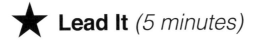 **Lead It** *(5 minutes)*

As the leader, choose to end your session in a way that suits the needs, dynamics, and vision of your group. The goal is to build trust and encourage vulnerability, both within the group and between individuals and God. You know your group best; choose the option that fits you!

1. CLOSING WITHOUT MINISTRY

- Flip the poster board around and on the back, have the word "IDENTITY" written.

- Explain that all 5 Power Beliefs help to shape who they are—their identity. This will be your transition to close and invite them back next week to discuss how our bodies work—further understanding our bodies and ourselves.

2. SMALL GROUPS CLOSING

- Flip the poster board around and on the back, have the word "IDENTITY" written.

- Have them break up in groups of 3–5 people.

- Use Reflection/Connection Points above.

3. MINISTRY TIME CLOSING

- Flip the poster board around and on the back, have the word "IDENTITY" written.

- Invite them to respond by making a new commitment to live in these power beliefs. You can have them come forward for a time of prayer and encounter.

- Or ask them to take some time to consider the reflection questions. Encourage them to journal their thoughts. Pray over them at the end.

* Optional small group time.

** Optional homework or encounter time for the student to do on his/her own.

03 LESSON THREE SEX+THE BODY PT.1

TEACHING GUIDE

This lesson introduces the connection between the body, soul, and spirit of every human being. Before we can even dive into the sexual reality of our physical body and its responses, we believe it is vital to be aware that sex is a multi-dimensional experience. Because of this fact, it is impossible to teach on the physical part of sex while leaving out the spiritual and soul connections. When we are educated and informed in a holistic way, we are more prone to make better choices.

If you did not grow up in the church, you may have never been told that you are more than your physical body and soul (mind, will & emotions). Movies, songs, and literature all communicate there is far more to bonding than just a physical or sexual bond. Yet, they have failed to explain how and why those non-physical bonds take place. This leaves us vulnerable to bonding and attaching and feeling helpless to understand why we have such an intense connection.

 OBJECTIVES

1. Body, Soul, and Spirit
2. Part 1: The Body
   Functions and Needs

 SCRIPTURES

1 Thessalonians 5:23 (NASB.
Genesis 1:26–28 (MSG)
Matthew 19:4–6 (MSG)
Matthew 5:27–28 (MSG)
Proverbs 4:23 (NCV)
Proverbs 30:18–19

 SUPPLIES (OPTIONAL)

- Whiteboard
- Whiteboard Marker
- Poster Board
- Marker

In the second part of this study, we will discuss the biochemical reactions occurring as a result of our sex drive, as well as the effects these chemicals have in our bodies. Once we understand how our bodies respond to certain stimuli and what goes on "under the surface," we can better manage our boundaries and our sex drive. This understanding enables us to draw our own line for purity, rather than being externally controlled by moral "rules" or social expectation.

Speaking purely of the physical, we are all aware that different levels of intimacy exist. From holding hands, all the way to sexual intercourse, we all possess various levels of arousal. Of course feelings of "love and trust" are going to be released in any intimate man-woman interaction, but we are talking more specifically about sexual stimulation. For instance, cuddling may not cause any sexual stimulation for one person, but for another it may be an immediate turn-on. This is why it is so important each student understand they are powerful individuals who must know themselves and understand how their individual bodies work. Since only they experience the chemical reactions (or feelings) happening in their body, no one can draw a "purity line" for them—they have to draw it for themselves.

You may be thinking, "The Bible has a very clear purity line," and it does. However, the level of sexual sin ranges from looking at someone with lust, to sex outside of marriage, but let's be honest...there's a lot in between. The Bible is very clear about sexual immorality, but leaves out the majority of "physical standards". We see God again giving us the power of choice and the power to listen to Him. We learn how to responsibly be aware of our bodies. Knowing how our bodies are made, caring for them well, and avoiding harm is extremely important...including sexual sins against our bodies. God will always be pursuing our hearts rather than controlling our behavior. We must however, take full responsibility and understand the potential consequence of our choices.

The next two lessons will focus on understanding your spirit, soul and body needs. Today we will focus on the physical body and its endorphins—the chemicals responsible for pleasure—that are released during ANY sexual activity:

> DEFINE IT: "Oxytocin" the chemical responsible for trust between partners and pair-bonding]

> DEFINE IT: "Vasopressin" the chemical responsible for commitment and responsibility]

Therefore, masturbation, "fingering", groping, French kissing, even sexual thoughts—anything that arouses us—bonds us to that person, picture, or fantasy.

We want to hand the ownership and responsibility back over to the students. It is their job to manage their own lives—no one else's; but until that lifestyle is driven from an inner belief system based on truth and power, the fight to value and protect their sexuality will remain uncontrolled.

Welcome/Introduction *(10 minutes)*

Welcome to week three! This week we get really honest and clear about sex and how to meet our physical and sexual needs in a healthy way! What you may not realize is that as men and women have distinct and unique needs that affect us differently. When we understand how our bodies operate, we no longer feel like there is "something wrong with us," as if we are the "only one" experiencing these feelings, thoughts, emotions. etc. This realization exposes that having sexual/physical responses (feeling "turned-on," feeling "connected" to another person, feeling "in love") is NORMAL and nothing to be afraid or ashamed of, but rather, something to be understood and managed.

There is more to sex than just having sex. This is why you can't just forget about someone you have given yourself to in an intimate way. It's the same reason you feel a pulling connection that can't be seen or explained but it's still there. Sex has many different realities and it moves us in more than just a physical way. It creates a deep soul tie, effecting both our spirit and soul to the core. God created sex to be much more than a physical act and we are going to explore this together for the next two weeks.

 Learn It *(30 minutes)*

1. BODY, SOUL, AND SPIRIT

You are made up of three parts. A body, a soul, and a spirit.

- *Your Spirit*—until we invite Jesus into our hearts, our spirits are dead to God; but once we accept Jesus into our heart, our spirits begin to experience, enjoy, and talk with the Holy Spirit (God) who then lives inside you. (Ephesians 2:3, Romans 8:10)

> ◉ **ILLUSTRATION OPTION**
>
> **Deflated Balloon Analogy:** Our spirit is like a deflated balloon that sits inside of us. Only when the Holy Spirit comes in does it fill up and become active inside of us.

- *Your Soul*—Includes your mind, will, and emotions. Your thoughts come from your mind. Your feelings come from your emotions. Your determination and decisions come from your will. Therefore, even though our soul is invisible, we know it exists because we can experience it. It makes up your personality— those distinctive characteristics that make you "you".

- *Your Body*—this is the literal flesh and bones (the physical body that we can touch and see), including the organs and physiological systems working within the body.

The Bible talks about all 3 parts:

I Thessalonians 5:23, "Now may the God of peace Himself sanctify you entirely; and may your spirit and soul and body be preserved complete, without blame at the coming of our Lord Jesus Christ." (See Hebrews 4:12, Matthew 16:24–26, Romans 1:9)

- Although you may ignore or be unaware of one of these "parts," you can't just "turn off" or separate yourself from any one of them.

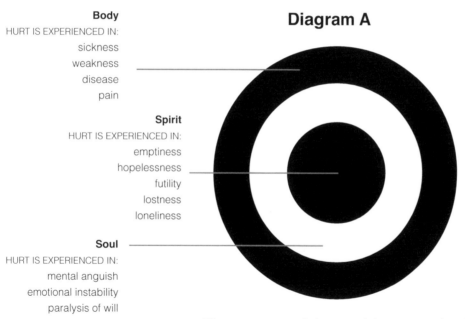

Diagram A

Body
HURT IS EXPERIENCED IN:
sickness
weakness
disease
pain

Spirit
HURT IS EXPERIENCED IN:
emptiness
hopelessness
futility
lostness
loneliness

Soul
HURT IS EXPERIENCED IN:
mental anguish
emotional instability
paralysis of will

The source of the problem may be in any of these three realms, but the hurt affects the whole person.

 **ILLUSTRATION OPTION**

Target "Bulls Eye": Bring your lesson to life by illustrating the body/soul/spirit reality!

Use poster board and a marker. Draw three large circles on the board, one inside of the other, so they resemble a "bull's-eye." Before the lesson begins, prep these materials and write "SEX" across all three circles on one side of the paper.

On the other side, draw the same three circles. Label the innermost circle 'spirit' the next 'soul', and the outermost 'body'. Use directional arrows to show 'living from the inside out' or 'outside in'. Get creative! Ask which part of the target the Holy Spirit lives in. Draw Him in the diagram! (see scriptures listed, for reference)

- *The idea:* You can't separate the "parts" of yourself any more than you can separate God from all of you!

2. YOUR SEX DRIVE

Having a sex drive simply means that you want to have sex with someone. It's very normal and nothing to be ashamed of—in fact, God gave you your sex drive! If you're alive, chances are you have one!

God gave you a sex drive for three specific reasons
(The three "B's"):

- To Makes **Babies**

  Genesis 1:26–28 (MSG) God spoke: "Let us make human beings in our image, make them reflecting our nature so they can be responsible for the fish in the sea, the birds in the air, the cattle, and, yes, Earth itself, and every animal that moves on the face of Earth." God created human beings; he created them godlike, reflecting God's nature. He created them male and female. God blessed them: "Prosper! Reproduce! Fill Earth! Take charge! Be responsible for fish in the sea and birds in the air, for every living thing that moves on the face of Earth."

- To **Bond** Intimately

  Matthew 19:4–6 (MSG) "Haven't you read in your Bible that the Creator originally made man and woman for each other, male and female? And because of this, a man leaves his father and mother and is firmly bonded to his wife, becoming one flesh—no longer two bodies but one. Because God created this organic union of the two sexes, no one should desecrate His art by cutting them apart."

- To Show God's **Beauty**

  Proverbs 30:18–19 "There are three things that are too amazing for me, four that I do not understand:the way of an eagle in the sky, the way of a snake on a rock, the way of a ship on the high seas, and the way of a man with a young woman."

 ILLUSTRATION OPTION

Glued Boards: Sex makes a man and woman "one." It glues them together. Bring your lesson to life by gluing two pieces of boards together. Explain the "oneness" that sex creates. Show that when you try to pull the pieces apart, it's very difficult and once you do, it leaves splinters in each piece.

3. UNDERSTANDING SEX

DEFINE IT: "Sex" intercourse between two people—vaginal, anal, and oral

- Sex takes place on more than the physical level. At the point of arousal, the brain releases endorphins and hormones making sex enjoyable, bonding, and addictive.[1]

---

1 Perl, L. (2013, June). Your brain on sex: 4 ways to use human physiology in your bedroom. Retrieved from http://www.yourtango.com/2013185203/your-brain-sex-4-ways-use- human-physiology-your-bedroom/page/2

- During sexual arousal, the "reason and behavior control" center shuts down in your brain for both men and women—resulting in the narrowed focus until climax is reached, via orgasm.[2]

- As the "control center" shuts down, the brain becomes governed by the cerebral cortex—the "center" responsible for attention, awareness, thought processing, and memory.

- This explains why our thoughts are overtaken by the other person and why we never forget the people we have sex with. **Memories are built during sex.**

- Chemicals and Responses: What's happening on the Biological Level?[3]

A. **ENDORPHINS** (DOPAMINE AND SEROTONIN)—THE "HAPPY" CHEMICALS

- These chemicals cause an intense rush of pleasure.

- They also enable our ability to focus and concentrate.

- Dopamine is also known as the "reward" hormone, releasing pleasure, and causing the desire to do it over again.

 **OPENING VIDEO OPTION 1**

Paul Blart: Mall Cop
Beauty Crash

Video Description:
While checking out a beautiful girl, Paul rides his scooter headfirst into a parked minivan.

 **OPENING VIDEO OPTION 1**

2 5 brain chemicals in healthy sexual act and how it is different from pornography addiction. (2012, Nov 01). Retrieved from http://www.feedtherightwolf.org/2010/11/brain-chemicals-in-healthy-sexual-act/

3 Freeman, S. (2008, Oct 07). What happens in the brain during an orgasm?. Retrieved from http://science.howstuffworks.com/life/human-biology/brain-during-orgasm2.htm

B. **OXYTOCIN**—THE "TRUST AND PAIR-BONDING" HORMONE[4]

- This hormone is what causes you to feel deeply bonded, or attached. *(Also released between a mother and her child)*

- It eases stress, creating feelings of "calm and closeness," which leads to increased trust. Women have a stronger reaction to oxytocin, in general.

- This is also the hormone that crystallizes emotional memories in our minds, making sex with another person very hard to forget.

C. **VASOPRESSIN**—THE "COMMITMENT" HORMONE[5]

- This hormone creates the desire to commit to our mate; creating loyalty.

- It inspires a protective sense; creating that "jealous" tendency.

- Drives us to protect our territory and offspring; heightening our sense of responsibility.

4. LEVELS OF INTIMACY— LOOKING, THINKING, TOUCHING

- Our bodies all respond to different levels of stimuli. Not just intercourse. Whether it's touching, looking at, or simply thinking about the opposite sex, you are creating intimacy that you will pattern throughout your life.

4 Salamon, M. (2010, Dec 10). 11 interesting effects of oxytocin. Retrieved from http://www.livescience.com/35219-11-effects-of-oxytocin.html

5 O'Brien, K. (2008, April 04). Oxytocin, vasopressin and a tale of two voles. Retrieved from http://thenewviewonsex.blogspot.com/2008/04/oxytocin-vasopressin-and-tale-of-two.htm

A. *LOOKING*—"LUSTING"

- **Looking Can Hurt You**

  Matthew 5:27–28 (MSG) "You know the next commandment pretty well, too: 'Don't go to bed with another's spouse.' But don't think you've preserved your virtue simply by staying out of bed. **Your heart can be corrupted by lust even quicker than your body.** Those leering looks you think nobody notices—they also corrupt."

- Lust destroys our ability to love by making us selfish. Love is about giving yourself to another person. Lust is about taking from another for self-satisfaction.

B. *THINKING*—"FANTASIZING"

DEFINE IT: "Fantasize" satisfying mental images.

- **Our thoughts are very powerful**

  Proverbs 23:7 (AMP) "For as he thinks in his heart, so is he…"

- **We can fantasize to fill a deeper void.**
- **Our thoughts determine our actions**

  Proverbs 4:23 (NCV) "Be careful what you think, because your thoughts run your life."

C. *TOUCHING*

DEFINE IT: "Touching" to come into or be in contact with.

- From holding hands to sexual intercourse, all physical interaction will release some level of chemical response in the body; the goal is to know your point of arousal.

5. DRAWING THE "LINE"

- Because we experience such a strong chemical response when sexually aroused, taking responsibility for our own sex drives is critical.

- No one can draw your "purity line" for you.

- We don't want to just "avoid having sex"; we want to honor our bodies, and steward our sex drives well. This is impossible to do without understanding our bodies, and why it's important to protect ourselves in the first place.

Conclusion: God created our bodies to bond with one another when engaging in sexual activity, revealing why He created it to only be experienced and enjoyed within the boundaries of marital covenant. Due to the chemicals released in our bodies when we physically interact with one another, our souls inherently begin to engage in the activity—which leads us into next week. God created sex to bond a husband and wife physically, emotionally (soul), and spiritually.

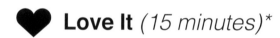 **Love It** *(15 minutes)**

REFLECTION TIME *(Personal)*

- Have you had a previous sexual experience (sexual encounter, pornography, masturbation, etc.) that left you with a pulling connection? Don't worry... there is nothing wrong with you. It's normal for you to feel bonded to that thing. Take a moment and invite the Holy Spirit into the experience. Ask Him to help you break any unhealthy connection you may have.

- Do you find yourself fantasizing (sexual or non-sexual) in order to fill a deeper void? How can you invite God into this area of your life and allow Him to fill these voids?

CONNECTION QUESTIONS *(small group)*

- Is it a new concept for you to think your sex drive is given to you by God? Does this at all change your view on sex?

- Have you used your 'power of choice' when it comes to your purity this year? Give an example.

- As we've talked about sex being a spirit, soul, and body experience, have you seen this to be true in your life? If not yours personally, have you seen it in a friend's life?

 Live It *(15 minutes)***

1. MY LIFE—We talked about your God given ability to create your own 'purity line'. Take a moment this week and invite God to show you yours. Make sure you get a chance to write it down somewhere.

2. MY FRIENDS—Find one or two trustworthy friends (mentors, youth leaders, etc.) to hold you accountable to your purity lines, whether you're single or in a relationship.

3. MY WORLD—Pay attention to how the world displays its view on sex (media, movies, advertisements, etc.), and compare it to the truth of what you've learned in this lesson about sex.

 ILLUSTRATION OPTION

Target "Bulls Eye": Use the "bull's-eye" you created earlier to illustrate this point! Flip over your poster board to reveal "SEX" written through all of the parts—body, soul and spirit!

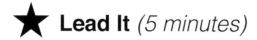 **Lead It** *(5 minutes)*

1. CLOSING WITHOUT MINISTRY

- Summarize: All of you is involved in sex, and sex affects all of you. You can't separate your body from your soul and spirit.

2. SMALL GROUPS CLOSING

- Have them break up in groups of 3–5 people.
- Use Reflection/Connection Points above.

3. MINISTRY TIME CLOSING

- Explain that some of them have never talked to God about how he made their bodies. Encourage them to take a moment to start the conversation with Him about having a purity plan in their life.

- Ask them to take some time to consider the reflection questions. Encourage them to journal their thoughts.

- Have them ask God if they have heard Him say anything to them about what we've talked about today. Pray over them, asking God to reveal the truth to them.

---

* Optional small group time.

** Optional homework or encounter time for the student to do on his/her own.

04 LESSON FOUR SEX+THE BODY PT.2

TEACHING GUIDE

Last week, we discussed the scientific relationship between our sex drives and our bodies. Sex was created as a gift for us to experience one of the most precious levels of intimacy here on earth. But how? We briefly touched on this in Lesson 3 by explaining the cause and the effect of the chemical response we experience from sexual stimulation. This week, we will be talking about the needs of the body, the soul, and the spirit and how to meet those needs in a healthy way.

Just as your physical body has very real needs—food, water, air—in order to stay alive, your soul and your spirit also have very real needs that need acknowledging and addressing in order for us to experience the abundant life God promised. (John 10:10) Yet even with this fool-proof plan to a happy, successful life, it is always a choice! We are responsible for knowing what we need and powerfully taking ownership of those needs.

This lesson introduces the fact that God created us with the capacity to manage our thoughts, our appetites, and our behaviors through

 OBJECTIVES

1. Body, Soul, Spirit Review
2. Part 2: Basic Human Needs: Body-Soul-Spirit
3. Living from Our Spirit

 SCRIPTURES

1 Cor 6:19; Rom 8:14–16
Gal 5:16–21; 1 John 4:4
Heb 4:12
Isaiah 58:11, VOICE
Phil 4:19, VOICE
3 John 1:2

 SUPPLIES (OPTIONAL)

- Whiteboard
- Whiteboard Marker
- Poster Board
- Marker

successfully managing the needs of our body, our soul, and our spirit. But where do we start? First, we must recognize that our soul's needs for intimacy, connection and comfort are very real and they will find a way to get met—whether through external (physical) or internal (spiritual) means. We are in danger of finding ourselves forming comfort habits such as overeating or pornography. This is where addressing the need of our spirit becomes vital. Constant connection with God establishes our identity and allows us to be completely seen, known, loved, valued, cared for, and protected. Because God is eternal and limitless, this relationship with Him is the only way to meet the critical needs of our soul for intimacy, connection, and comfort.

As a triune being, we must be aware that our body, soul and spirit are interacting with each other all the time. God created the body (external experience) to positively affect the soul and spirit (internal experience) and vice versa. In other words, human relationships, food, exercise, entertainment and other external resources, are intended to enhance our experience in our bodies, relationships, and hearts. However, when we choose to ignore our connection with God, these become the only sources for intimacy, connection, and comfort in our lives. We start to abuse them by trying to get more from them than they can give us. Because we are eternal beings, such limited and temporary resources will never be able to fully satisfy us. This is why God encourages us to live from the inside out having our spirit connected with His Spirit first.

We wrap up this lesson by providing tools that enable you to begin living from your spirit and embrace the journey of allowing God to lead your heart to connection with Him. Everyone's relationship with Him is going to look different and carry unique tools for connection, but we want to encourage you that it is never too late to begin! By walking through this journey in power and community, we disarm fear and shame, creating an environment of celebration and freedom!

Welcome/Introduction *(10 minutes)*

Let's review the Body-Soul-Spirit analogy from our previous lesson! The "Bull's Eye" gives a visual representation of how we are made; consisting of 3 main parts. Last time we covered a very specific element of the body—our sex drives. We discussed how God wired our sex drives to respond to various interactions with the opposite sex. We looked at the chemical responses that directly cause emotional attachments, and how we can get our physical needs (sexual intimacy) met in a healthy way.

Today we are going to take you deeper into the target, explaining the basic human needs of the body, soul, and spirit. Each part has specific needs but, when those needs go unmet, our bodies begins to rule our lives, trying to compensate for a lack of intimacy and connection. Our job is to first recognize that our spirit and soul have needs. We must then cultivate an environment around us to proactively meet these needs in a positive way. Most of us are aware that our bodies and our souls have needs. We consciously experience these on a daily basis, but the needs of our spirit are even more important to understand and care for. Ignoring the needs of our spirits is not only ignorant, but dangerous; on the contrary, focusing *solely* on our spirits, and neglecting the needs of our bodies and our souls, is just as harmful.

We all long for deep intimacy, real connection, and loving comfort. In order to fill this void, God created us as a body-soul-spirit, triune being—like Himself. We are able to connect and communicate with His Spirit through our own spirit and experience the intimacy, connection, and comfort we need. When these needs are being met, we are able to more powerfully take care of our external world; including our thoughts, appetites, and emotions. Living from our spirits is not only possible it is most beneficial! Understanding this internal structure enables us to live successful and satisfying lives!

 **Learn It** *(30 minutes)*

A. REVIEW LAST WEEK
*Refer back to Target Illustration

1. Last week we discussed the scientific relationship between our bodies and our sex drives. (Review as much as desired.)

   Examples:

   - Our sex drive is a BLESSING—given by God—meant to be managed BEFORE and AFTER marriage.

   - At the point of arousal, our brain releases chemicals that create emotional bonds.

   - Those chemicals—dopamine, oxytocin, and vasopressin—are addictive and rewarding.

1. This week we will discuss our most basic human needs: what it takes to meet them in a healthy way, and what happens when these needs go unmet.

Basic Human Needs

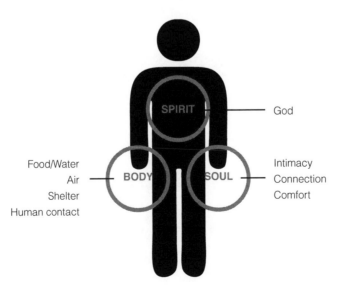

2. All three "parts" (body, soul and spirit) are necessary to understand and manage. With proper care, our spiritual health will fulfill the most basic needs of our soul, allowing us to enjoy our physical needs without abusing them.

B. THE BODY: PART 2

INTRO: We are made up of 3 parts—body, soul, spirit—and each part has needs.

DEFINE IT: "Physical Make-up" our flesh and bones; 5 senses— touch, sight, hearing, smell, taste

1. BODY

a. In order to physically survive, our human body *needs*[1] :

- Food
- Water
- Air (Breathing)
- Shelter
- Human Contact
    - *Newborns denied physical contact with other humans can actually die from this lack of contact, even when provided with proper nutrition and shelter.*[2]

b. All other needs are secondary to these basic physiological needs, because you have to be *alive* to have needs. (AKA: We're not feeding dead people in the morgue or asking what they need.)

c. Healthily meeting these needs looks like the (healthy) body of a LIVING person. These needs enable *life*.

d. Abuse of these needs (due to excess or lack) can lead to physical illness, obesity, anorexia, etc.

---

1 McLeod, S. (2007) Maslow's Hierarchy of Needs. Retrieved from http://www. simplypsychology.org/maslow.html

2 Coila, B. (2013, Aug 13). The effect of human contact on newborn babies. Retrieved from http://www.livestrong.com/article/72120-effect-human-contact-newborn-babies/

2. SOUL

"Soul" the realm of every emotion we *feel*, every thought we *think*, and every decision or desire we're *driven* by. This is part of our inner world.

b. In order to *emotionally* thrive, our soul needs:

- Intimacy
- Connection
- Comfort

c. The interesting thing about our soul needs is that they are affected and met (to a degree) by our body and/or our spirit.

- For example, as we discussed last week, the chemicals released in our brain (dopamine, oxytocin, and vasopressin) actually cause emotional bonds. Enabling us to experience intimacy, connection, and comfort solely due to a physical reaction.

d. Interestingly, sex is not the only stimulant of these bonding and "feel-good" chemicals. The following external resources are just a few other stimulants[3,4]

- Exciting activity: competition, sex, cliff jumping, etc.
- Laughter
- Exercise: runner's "high"
- Food
- Physical contact (not sexual)
- A good flick—emotional movies/shows
- Human interaction/connection
- Drugs, Alcohol, etc.

3 Haller, M. (2012, Mar 07). The surprising benefits of a hot shower. Retrieved from http://news.menshealth.com/unleash-your-brains-happy-chemical/2012/03/07

4 McIlhaney, J. S., & Bush, F. M. (2008). Hooked: New science on how casual sex is affecting our children. Chicago: Northfield Publishing.

5 Sack, D. D. (n.d.). Alcohol releases "feel-good" chemicals in your brain. Retrieved from http://www.promises.com/articles/alcohol-brain-chemicals

e. Because these stimulants release the chemicals that make us "feel" comforted and connected, sometimes we try to meet the needs of our soul only through physical means (e.g. relationships, casual sex, eating, exercise, etc.)

f. None of these stimulants are inherently bad. The abuse (excess) of these activities is what leads to an unhealthy, addicted lifestyle.

▶ OPENING VIDEO OPTION 1

g. The other side of this "unhealthy heart" scenario can look like a person who has shut down their emotions and convinced themselves that they don't need a healthy balance of any of these things above.

▶ OPENING VIDEO OPTION 2

Our spirit also affects and meets the needs of our soul through our connection with God.

h. It is important and necessary to understand that both our body and our spirit was created to healthily affect our soul. Because our physical resources are temporary and limited, the key is allowing our spirit (filled with Holy Spirit) to be the **primary source** of meeting our soul's needs.

VIDEO OPTION 1

Paul Blart: Mall Cop – Internet Dating Video

In this scene, Paul Blart is excessively consuming food (sweets) and trying to keep busy with his job to deal with his loneliness (due to lack of relationships and connection). *End video at 1:54*

VIDEO OPTION 2

How the Grinch Stole Christmas – Everything I Need

In this scene the Grinch passes the time away alone, trying to assure him that he has everything he needs inside his cave. He is independent and doesn't need anything outside his own world.

i. Healthily meeting these needs looks like a person with good boundaries, who is managing their relationships well and getting their needs met from God before anything else (which we will cover next). This enables them to not abuse the external sources (relationships, food, sex, etc. in their lives, but rather use them as tools for enhancing their lives.

3. SPIRIT

DEFINE IT: "Spirit" The place of connection with God where His Spirit lives within us

a. In order for us to *spiritually* thrive, our spirit, first and foremost, needs one thing: God.

b. The sole purpose of God giving us our spirits was to allow us to have relationship with Him on an individual basis.

c. Our connection with God meets our deepest/truest levels of intimacy, identity, comfort, and connection.

  i. Only through building and sustaining relationship with God can we fully experience the sufficiency of these needs.

How do we start? By (first) believing that Jesus is the Son of God and inviting Him into our hearts. Then, by receiving and responding to His unconditional love for us, hearing and following His voice, recognizing and enjoying His Presence, etc.

  ii. We maintain connection and communication with Him through communion, worship, prayer, Bible study, and relationship with other believers.

  iii. Healthily meeting the needs of our spirit leads us to be **confident** and **self-aware**. *Christ* is the source of our identity. We are able to go into relationships ready to *give*, rather than only seeking to *get*.

4. LIVING BY OUR SPIRIT

a. When we are born-again, our spirits house the Holy Spirit which enables us to have a personal relationship with God. (*see 1 Cor 6:19; Rom 8:14–16*)

b. Once we are filled with His Spirit, we are connected to the Source that is willing AND able to meet our soul's needs. Utilizing that Source is a *choice*. (*see Gal 5:16*)

c. When we choose to let God meet the needs of our souls, we are able to powerfully manage external resources of comfort, connection, and intimacy and not be controlled by them. (*see Phil 4:19, VOICE; 1 John 4:4*)

d. As our spirit (connection with God) prospers, our soul prospers; as our soul prospers, our body prospers. (*see 3 John 1:2*)

Conclusion: Our souls respond directly to whatever we are feeding on spiritually. In other words, when we are in relationship with and listening to the Holy Spirit, our thoughts, emotions, and desires begin to reflect His—and become healthy and holy. When we are not living by our spirit and exclusively try to meet our soul's needs through external means, our thoughts, emotions, and desires become toxic and destructive. It leaves us feeling unsatisfied and incomplete. Thankfully, we have alternative methods to meeting our soul's deepest needs through relationship with God.

Next week we will be discussing Restoration and the supernatural power of choice and forgiveness. We are all growing in each season of our lives and we are excited to come alongside you in this journey of purity and walk it out in community and power.

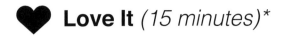 Love It *(15 minutes)**

REFLECTION TIME *(Personal)*

- Do you find yourself ignoring one or all of these areas of need: body (physical needs), soul (emotional feelings), or spirit (talking to God needs)? What can you do differently to make sure all of these needs are getting met in a healthy way?

- You are in a process of learning to understand your needs and desires and developing healthy skills for meeting them in relationships. Along this journey, it's totally normal to make mistakes and learn by trial and error. How do you currently handle your mistakes? Do you punish yourself? Do you talk about it with your community? Journal your response.

CONNECTION QUESTIONS *(Small Group)*

- What are 2 or 3 things you can implement in your life to begin or maintain constant connection with God and to start living from your spirit?

- Do you recognize any areas in your life that you are abusing external resources to try to get your needs met? If so, what can you do differently to manage those needs?

- What does it look like to live as a triune (body, soul, spirit) being?

Live It *(15 minutes)***

1. MY LIFE—This week, find ways to connect with each part of your being (body, soul, spirit). For example, spend time with the Lord to meet the needs of you spirit. Go for a walk, or exercise to help meet the needs of your physical body. Hang out with your closest friends or watch a funny movie to fulfill your soul needs.

2. MY FRIENDS—Challenge your friends this week to bring their full selves to the table in your conversations. Find out how this will affect not only your personal life, but also your friendships. Then relate this to being a healthy body, soul and spirit.

3. MY WORLD—Observe the world around you, whether it be school, your family, or tv shows, and notice how they fulfill their needs when they are feeling alone or frustrated. Compare that to what you learned this week.

 Lead It *(5 minutes)*

1. CLOSING WITHOUT MINISTRY

- Summarize: All of you are involved in sex, and sex affects all of you. You can't separate your body from your soul and spirit.

2. SMALL GROUPS CLOSING

- Have them break up in groups of 3–5 people.
- Use Reflection/Connection Points above.

3. MINISTRY TIME CLOSING

- Explain
- Ask them to take some time to consider the reflection questions. Encourage them to journal their thoughts.
- Have them ask God if they have heard Him say anything to them about what we've talked about today. Pray over them, asking God to reveal the truth to them.

* Optional small group time.

** Optional homework or encounter time for the student to do on his/her own.

05 LESSON FIVE SEX & RESTORATION

TEACHING GUIDE

Last week, we discussed the importance of managing the needs of our body, our soul, and our spirit. We explained how living from your spirit (through connection with God) is the only way to live a truly whole and successful life.

We understand that many people have never heard this information before and may be beginning this journey for the first time. We want to celebrate that victory! Simply choosing to embrace a new way of thinking is the first battle won in this life-long war for our purity. Purity actually means "freedom from anything that debases, contaminates, or pollutes." Therefore, the war for our purity is not merely sexual. Rather, because of our love for God and our desire to know Him, we strive to keep our hearts and our minds uncontaminated—from fear, jealousy, lies, and anything else the enemy tries to use to get us to meet our needs outside of God. Due to the nature of the curriculum, our focus today will be on sexual purity; however, keep in mind that our sexuality is only part of what "purity" encompasses.

 OBJECTIVES

1. Spirit Restoration
2. Soul (Mind, Emotions & Will) Restoration
3. Body (Physical) Restoration

 SCRIPTURES

Ps. 51:4a
Heb 7:27 (NCV)
Rom 8:39 (NCV)
Hos 4:12 (NET)
Rev 3:19
Matt 4:24MSG
Acts 10:38 (VOICE)

 SUPPLIES (OPTIONAL)

- Mobile phone, cord, power source

In this lesson, we are going to break down how restoration was meant for all three parts of our being: our body, our soul and our spirit. We know from scriptures like Psalm 51 (which King David wrote after sinning sexually with Bathsheba) that when we confess and repent of our sin before God, He renews our spirit and our connection with Him is restored! God didn't send His only Son Jesus to die a terrible death on the cross to have just one part of you (your spirit) restored. Because of the life, death, and resurrection of Jesus Christ, we can be restored from physical sickness, chemical imbalances (caused by sex, alcohol, drug use etc), pain (emotional and physical), regret and internal scars. God works all things for the good of those who love Him! Therefore, the biggest message we want to send today is HOPE. Not just for restoration of our spiritual connection with God, but restoration of our whole being!

Because we are dealing with sexual restoration today, we want to be clear in communicating that the result of sex was never meant to be bad, negative, or painful. However, many people experience unhealthy addiction, unhealthy soul-ties, STIs, unwanted pregnancies, and physical damage through sex. Some through no fault of their own (abuse, rape etc) and others by their own choice (curiosity, peer pressure, desire etc). If these outcomes are real, then why are people still willing to take the risk? Because God designed sex as beautiful! Sex is bonding! Sex is life-giving! Outside of marriage, people will still experience this beautiful, bonding, life-giving side to sex. The problem lies in the lack of commitment, more specifically, the lack of covenant with one another; because covenant says, "I am in this for the long haul. I will always choose you. I will put you before me. What's mine is yours." The rejection and the abandonment of such life, connection, and beauty (that sex creates) will destroy our hearts, distort our emotions, devalue our worth, dislodge our connection with God, and demand a response (good or bad). This reality makes it obvious why God created sex to be enjoyed only within the covenant of marriage.

In dealing with the topic of sexual restoration, the last thing we want to do is shame sex. Our goal is to create a greater value for sex and discuss its effect on our entire being. In this process, we disarm shame and reignite hope and vision! This lesson concludes by reminding our audience, and ourselves, that God offers forgiveness and a fresh start to each one of us. At every moment. No one is past redemption.

Welcome/Introduction *(10 minutes)*

Today we are going to get very practical about restoration. God always meant for us to experience full redemption, which includes your body, your soul, and your spirit.

The dictionary defines restoration as "the action of returning something to a former condition; the process of repairing or renovating; the act of reinstating something back to its original form or function"

In the aftermath of his sin with Bathsheba, King David went to the Lord and asked Him to give him a new heart, renew a "steadfast spirit" in him and restore his joy. The Hebrew root word for renew and restore is the verb 'chadash', meaning to renew oneself, repair, restore or even to polish a sword until it gleams! The root word for steadfast is 'niphal' meaning to be firm, stable and established; securely determined, enduring. We are saying "Lord, renew my ability to be stable, restore my shine!"

As you now know through our previous teachings, sex affects our bodies through physical contact, chemical release, emotional bonding, and many other things. These effects were designed to strengthen and enhance our connection with another human being.

Unfortunately, for centuries people have tried to use sex (all sexual activity) to meet their deepest needs for intimacy and connection. When practiced outside of the marriage covenant, this can end up resulting in unhealthy soul ties, unwanted pregnancies and sexually transmitted infections (STI). When we put something or someone else at the "center stage" of our lives, it deeply affects our relationship with God, because that place belongs to Him. He gives us identity and meets our deepest desire and need for intimacy.

Jesus Christ came to earth and died on a cross so that we could have a full and happy life! The blood of Jesus washes away bad decisions, forgets past mistakes, and restores moments of abuse. His death paid the price for our sin; Jesus received the punishment that we deserved. The good news doesn't end there! God said that anyone who believes that Jesus is the Son of God is saved from hell, adopted into His family, and made a NEW creation! Consequently, that adoption into the Family creates access to the supernatural reality of heaven, enabling us to experience awakening in our spirits, healing in our bodies, and comfort in our souls! That is the reality of relationship with Jesus Christ! That is just a glimpse of the hope and the healing that Jesus has made available.

Today we will discuss the spirit-soul-body effects of premarital sex, its harmful outcomes, and the hope that God has provided for our restoration. Contrary to previous lessons, today we will address our spirit, more specifically its hope for restoration, before discussing our physical and emotional/mental healing. When our connection with God is restored, we are able to readily pull on Him for the healing and restoration of our body and our soul. Every bad choice is redeemable, and no one is without hope.

 **Learn It** *(30 minutes)*

RESTORATION

A. SPIRIT Restoration

1. Premarital sex affects our spirit, because it's a sin.

   • It's a sin against God and our own body (Ps 51:4; 1 Cor. 6:16–20 [MSG]).

2. Our sin once separated us from God.

   a. In the Old Testament when the Israelites sinned, it separated them (Isa 59:2) and only offerings and sacrifices reconnected them.

   b. Our sin (before belief in Jesus) did separate us (Eph 2:12).

   c. Jesus made the 'once-and-for-all' sacrifice for us (Heb 7:27) so once we have chosen to believe in Jesus it is impossible for God to separate himself from us.

   d. When we choose to sin we are turning our backs on God and how many know that when we do that to anyone, we disconnect from them. Our fellowship with them is broken.

3. Sin is the result of believing a lie.

   a. In our choice to sin we choose to turn away from God, and in doing that we believe the lie that we are disconnected from Him when, in fact, He hasn't moved.

   b. The enemy leads us to question, "Did God really say...?" (Gen 3:1 [NIV]) (I.E. We don't believe Him.)

c. He will tell us that intimacy with God is not enough and convince us that we must have a sexual connection with someone to get that need met. When we do this we commit adultery or idolatry. (Hos 4:12 [NET]) (I.E. We replace Him)

d. We believe God separates Himself from us because we think He is afraid of our sin and can't handle it or we think He is angry. We are full of shame. (Gen 3:7 [NIV]) (I.E. We hide from Him.)

[It is important to differentiate areas of sin that we allow to grow into lifestyles, versus areas of genuine weakness that we are warring to overcome. It's the grace of God that empowers us to gain victory over areas of sin in our lives].

4. Repentance instantly restores our connection with God. (2 Chronicles 7:14)

a. The original Greek word for repentance is metanoia, which means: "'change of mind' and involves a turning with remorse from sin to God; making a 180 turn in direction. (I.E. we are choosing to turn back to Him.) (Rev 3:19)

b. God responds to our initiation. Therefore, simply turning our thoughts towards Him begins that reconnection. (James 4:8–10)

c. God is ready and wanting to forgive us and restore our spirit—connection with Him back to where it was before we sinned. (1 John 1:9)

- Extravagant forgiveness is God's idea. (Matt 18:21–22)

- Forgiveness restores the standard.

Power Source, Cord, & Phone: Use any cord and power source to illustrate how the function and purpose of the cord doesn't change when disconnected from the power source, it simply becomes ineffectual. In the same way, when we are separated/disconnected from the Lord (due to sin), our effectiveness ends, and we are no longer able to transfer the life and power we once could when connected to the Source.

Our access to the Source never changes, but we have the choice to repent and reconnect or to continue in sin and remain stagnant.

B. SOUL Restoration

1. Mind—Your Thoughts and Beliefs

a) Whether you realize it or not, premarital sex changes the way you think about yourself and the way you view the world.

b) Harmful outcomes

(1) Lies & False Beliefs

- eg. I am not worth the wait, the commitment, or the protection.

- eg. I am a victim to my hormones and temptations.

- eg. I'll never get married; marriage doesn't last.

- eg. Marriage is just a "piece of paper."

- eg. I am stuck in this situation/relationship.

c) Hope and restoration

(1) Truth sets you free. *(John 8:32)*

(2) You can control your thoughts. *(2 Cor 10:5)*

(3) Renewing your mind leads to transformation. *(Rom 12:2)*

(4) Transformation is visible. *(Matt 7:16)*

Cycle of Freedom: God says that the truth will set you free; therefore, it is vital that we know the truth about ourselves, our worth, marriage, and life in general! We begin this journey to freedom by knowing the Word of God, and reminding ourselves of who we are (see Lesson 2). We then realize that as we take control of our thoughts (choosing not to give in to temptation) and renew our minds with truth (demolishing lies by choosing to believe what God says instead), we begin living differently. Others see this transformation by our choices, the way we value/respect ourselves and others, our level of hope, etc. This cycle becomes a lifestyle, enabling perpetual health and freedom.

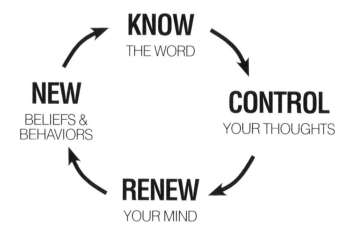

KNOW
THE WORD

CONTROL
YOUR THOUGHTS

RENEW
YOUR MIND

NEW
BELIEFS &
BEHAVIORS

2. Will—Your Desires and Decisions

a) Premarital sex looks desirable when we don't understand it. The reality is that we don't crave the action of "sex" as much as we crave what it offers. The pleasure, excitement and connection (that sex produces) make it desirable.

b) Hope & restoration

(1) God does not tempt you. (James 1:13)

(a) Tempt means "to cause (someone) to do or want to do something even though it may be wrong, bad, or unwise."

(i) The enemy dresses himself up as something desirable, but it's deceiving. (2 Cor 11:14–15)

(ii) The enemy only comes to steal, kill and destroy. (John 10:10a) Therefore, anything he's tempting us with can only result in destruction.

(2) You are not defined by the temptations that you resist, but by the values that you embrace.

(a) Jesus was tempted in every way! (Heb 4:15)

(b) There is no temptation that we can't overcome. (1 Cor 10:13)

(3) We become what we behold. (2 Cor 3:18)

(a) As we spend time with the Lord, we become more like Him. As such, His desires become our desires; and vice versa! If it matters to you, it matters to Him.

3. Emotion

a) Premarital sex affects our soul by keeping us unhealthily attached to people we are not in covenant with.

b) Soul Ties

   (1) Define: the emotional bond between two people created through time investment, life exchange, and commitment.

   (2) Soul-ties are healthy when they involve covenant and commitment, and dangerous when formed outside of God's guidelines.

   (3) Jonathan and King David = healthy soul tie.
   (1 Sam 18:1 [NIV])

   (4) Sex Outside Marriage = unhealthy soul tie
   (1 Cor 6:16 [NIV])

   (5) Breaking unhealthy soul-ties

      (a) Repent of any sin. (eg: premarital sex)

      (b) Renounce any rash vows you made.
         (eg: "I will love you forever!")

      (c) Hope and restoration

         (1) Ask God to remove any curse spoken over you by that person. (eg: "No man will ever love you the way I loved you!")

         (2) Get rid of anything that was given to you by that person, if it keeps you emotionally attached to them. (eg: gifts, love letters, pictures etc)

         (3) Refer to "Breaking Soul Ties" prayer to lead individuals or your group in breaking unhealthy soul ties and restoring your emotions back to strength and hope.

C. BODY Restoration

1. Sex affects our physical bodies in a number of ways.

    a) Chemical release—rewarding and addictive

    b) Brain builds "muscle memory" (synapses) causing us to want to repeat the behavior.

    c) Sexually Transmitted Infections (possible)

    d) Ruptured hymens (females)

    e) Pregnancy

2. Hope and restoration

    a) Our brain's muscle memory is moldable from before birth until after death!***

    (1) By simply "starving out" old behavioral/mental thought patterns (by choosing new ones), one weakens the connections (in the brain) that make that behavior/thought/reaction so "normal" or automatic.

    b) God heals supernaturally.
    (Matt 4:24 [MSG], Acts 10:38 [VOICE])

    (1) Testimonies—the more personal, the better!

    (2) Hymen restored

    (3) STIs healed

Conclusion: There is no part of you—spirit, soul or body—that God cannot restore. No one is past redemption. Restoration is God's idea! You being a "new creation" was His plan! He is willing and able to take any of your mistakes and work it together for your good (Rom 8:28 [NIV]). Next week, we will discuss the good things God wants to plan with you for your life. We will get to work and talk about how you will plan to live your life in purity, and in covenant with God; loving yourself and others well!

***Often we feel like we are unable to change, that we're too far gone. We say things like, "That's just the way I am!" or, "I've always been this way, I can't change now!" But scientific research has discovered the truth that the human brain (and our behavior) is able to grow and change from the cradle to the grave.

In this excerpt from page 29 of the book "Hooked," Doctors McIlhaney and Bush explain how the brain changes: *"The primary things that change in the brain structure; that mold it, are its synapses. Synapses either are sustained or they are allowed to deteriorate based on behavior and experience. It may seem incredible, but the things we see, do, and experience actually cause part of our brains to flourish, i.e., synapses that survive and strengthen; and part of our brain to weaken, i.e., synapses that disintegrate or die."*

Simply put, synapses get stronger or weaker depending on whether or not they are used. When it comes to changing our behaviors, we find that the things we practice, or do regularly, become habits. Skills that we stop using, we become weaker at. This is because we are using or losing the synapses needed for these thought processes and actions. This means that when we encounter new circumstances or information, we are able to create new behaviors in reaction to it. If you choose to think differently, you will be able to act differently. Change is not a hopeless cause. You were created for it.

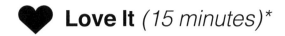 **Love It** *(15 minutes)**

REFLECTION TIME *(Personal)*

- Take some time and ask the Holy Spirit to reveal to you whether you are dealing with shame in any area of your life. Is it causing (or has it caused) you to hide from Him?

- Is there any area in your life that you want made new (restored)? If so, start dialoguing with God about it. Is there anything you need to talk to Him about and ask forgiveness for (repent)?

- Is there a destructive habit that you are dealing with? Having heard the information on scientific and supernatural hope for change, are you encouraged to know that you can partner with the Holy Spirit to strengthen your will (part of your soul) to bring freedom? Ask the Lord to show you the hope He has for you in that area. Spend some time thanking God for this.

CONNECTION QUESTIONS *(Small Group)*

- Were you aware of the power that God has to restore/ heal all of your being? How do you feel about the restoration process that was discussed in this lesson? Discuss with one another.

- Do you have habits or behaviors that you want to change? Do you feel like you can talk to God about them? Talk within the group or in pairs about why this might be.

- What can you do now to start taking steps to break old habits and establish new behaviors? Who can you share this with? Who can encourage you in your process?

Live It *(15 minutes)***

1. MY LIFE—Take time this week to journal and think about who you want to be in 10 years. What do you want to be known for? What theme is your story going to be shouting to the earth? Hope? Restoration? Overcoming? Purity? Justice? (etc.) Share this with one person in your life. Share this with the Lord and ask Him to give you the hope, courage and strength you need to become that person.

2. MY FRIENDS—Ask two friends in your small group how they are doing with their action plan. Call your mentor and connect at least once to let them know how you are doing.

3. MY WORLD—Find stories of people who have overcome in the areas of life that you have learned about in this lesson. (You can checkout www.moralrevolution.com for encouraging stories). Note how they did it.

★ **Lead It** *(5 minutes)*

1. CLOSING WITHOUT MINISTRY

   • Summarize Lesson: God wants to restore ALL of you— your body, your soul, and your spirit.

2. SMALL GROUPS CLOSING

   • Have them break up in groups of 3–5 people.

   • Use Reflection/Connection Points above.

3. MINISTRY TIME CLOSING

   • Explain that God is able to restore them spirit, soul and body.

- If you feel to, lead them through a prayer to renounce any soul ties. Encourage them to do this verbally, out loud, and in Jesus' name. Eg, "In Jesus' name, I now renounce any ungodly soul ties formed between myself and _____ as a result of _____ (fornication, etc.)."

- Lead them to break the soul tie in Jesus' name. Encourage them to do it out loud, using their authority in Jesus. Eg, "I now break and sever any ungodly soul ties formed between myself and_____ as a result of _____ (fornication, etc.) in Jesus' name."

- Have them ask God if they have heard Him say anything to them about what we've talked about today. Pray over them, asking God to reveal the truth to them.

* Optional small group time.

** Optional homework or encounter time for the student to do on his/her own.

06 LESSON SIX SEX & COVENANT

TEACHING GUIDE

Last week, we discussed the great hope we have in Christ Jesus; we are able to be fully restored—spirit, soul and body! It is possible to change and live a new life in our spirits and in our actions because of what Jesus has done and does for us and because of the way we were created (our chemical makeup and brain functions). We learned there is hope for us as we endeavor to live a life like Jesus—pure and blameless, without spot or blemish!

This week, we dive into the nitty-gritty of what it looks like and what it takes to be pure and blameless in our lives, particularly in our sexuality. This lesson has the potential to be a highly interactive lesson, should you choose to use the Purity Covenant and Purity Plan (attached as a curriculum resource).

Sexual purity can be a daunting and discouraging idea to some, who feel like they are stuck in patterns of unhealthy behaviors. Walking out of a lifestyle of sexual sin, or just maintaining a lifestyle of purity takes both your

 OBJECTIVES

1. Do You Have What It Takes? (Covenant)
2. Where Are You Going? (Purity Looks Like Something)
3. How Are You Going to Get There? (Purity Plan)

 SCRIPTURES

Proverbs 29:18 [VOICE]
1 Corinthians 5:17 [NIV]
1 Pet 2:9 [NIV]

 RESOURCES

Purity Covenant, Purity Plan

own willpower (your ability to choose what you will or will not do) and God's supernatural power. We need His grace, which enables us to do what we could not to do on our own. We get access to this when we enter into covenant with Him.

Being in covenant with God, we are able to receive the full supply of every bit of strength and resource He has, to do the impossible in our own lives. This kind of partnership is what Jesus died for! He sacrificed Himself and is coming back for a spotless Bride, who will rule and reign with Him. We have the honor and privilege of beginning to experience that kind of relationship with Him right now! We get to rule over ourselves with Him, in order to create the life that we're dreaming of!

This week, we help our students develop vision for what purity will look like in their own life, and make a plan for how they're going to get there! *"Where there is no vision from God, the people run wild, but those who adhere to God's instruction know genuine happiness" (Prov 29:18 [VOICE])*. Once they know where they want to go, (they know who they want to be and what they want to do, as explained in the Purity Covenant) they'll make their own Purity Plan to help them get there! We talk about the importance of inviting accountability into their process, to strengthen and encourage them on their journey. We discuss the pitfalls that we face when we try to just change our behaviors, and how to go after the roots of our behaviors. Change is an inside job and with God on our side, nothing is impossible!

Welcome/Introduction *(10 minutes)*

Last week, we discussed how God restores all of us from our past—no matter how bad it has been! We also learned that we are able to work with God to change the things we do. Many of us made the brave decision to invite God to make us new—body, soul and spirit! Congratulations! And today, you need to know that if you want it, God is still ready to meet you and to make things right with you, and for you!

If you've chosen to repent and ask God for forgiveness, if God has touched you in your body and soul, you need to know that you've been made new (1 Cor 5:17)! According to God, you are pure, right now. Remember, being pure is being free from anything that debases, contaminates, or pollutes. The Bible says it this way: *"You are a chosen people, a royal priesthood, a holy nation, God's special possession, that you may declare the praises of him who called you out of darkness into his wonderful light"* (1 Pet 2:9 [NIV]). The word "holy" here means to be set apart for God, to be exclusively for Him. If you are set apart, you are separate from the world—you are unmixed, uncontaminated, clear and pure![1]

God has made you pure, and the goal is to stay that way! Not that you'll never make mistakes (sin), but that you'll never let your mistakes define who you are and whose you are. You belong to God, and He's created you to be is pure, holy, and set apart for Him. He's rooting you on to a pure life—unmixed, undefiled by this world—looking like Jesus in everything you say and do!

This is where the rubber meets the road. If we want to stay pure, sexually and otherwise, we need to get into the game and begin to make choices to get ourselves from the starting line today, to the finish line of our lives with sexual purity and integrity. It is possible, but we desperately need God's grace and empowerment to do it!

Today we're going to talk about what it looks like to be in relationship with God in a way that we can work with Him and receive from Him all that we need to live a pure life, especially in our sexuality. We call this relationship covenant. We're also going to think about what it's going to take to actually DO what we want to do, which is to live a life of purity.

---

1 Strong's Concordance: "holy," Strong's G40 "hagios"

 **Learn It** *(30 minutes)*

COVENANT[2]

DEFINE IT: "Covenant" A binding promise made between two people[3].

DO YOU HAVE WHAT IT TAKES?

- A covenant ties you together with another person.

- Covenanters are in such close relationship with each other that all they have or possess in this life is available to each other upon request.[4]

- In Biblical times, this kind of promise could only be dissolved if one of the covenanters died.[5] It is a life-long promise that binds you together for one common purpose.

2 [Source for information on "Covenant," unless otherwise cited.] Kenyon, E. W. (1969). The blood covenant. (23 ed., pp. 10–22). Lynnwood: Kenyon's Gospel Publishing. Retrieved from http://hopefaithprayer.com/books/TheBloodCovenant-Kenyon.pdf

3 http://www.merriam-webster.com/dictionary/covenant

4 Nelson, W. (2003, May 30). Understanding the blood covenant [Online forum comment]. Retrieved from http://www.faithwriters.com/article-details.php?id=4089

5. Jones, D. W. & Tarwater, J. K. (2005, September 18). Are biblical covenants dissoluble?: toward a theology of marriage Reformed Perspectives Magazine, 7(38), 5–6. Retrieved from http://myseminary.org/articles/dav_jones/th.tarwater.jones.covenants.pdf

Old Testament

a. God and Abraham *(Genesis 15–17)*

b. God made a covenant with Abraham that tied Him together with Abraham, and the whole Israelite nation after him.

c. The covenant? *"I will be your God, you will be My people."* *(Gen 17:7–8, Ex 6:7, Jer 7:23)*

d. People used blood in making covenants. God told Abraham to kill an animal in His place. Abraham shed his own blood by being circumcised. *(Gen 15:9–10, Gen 17:10–11)*

e. The blood symbolized that each person was choosing to "die" for the other—that each would give up their own life to make the other successful and to keep their own part of the covenant.

New Testament

a. Jesus and Me (and The Church)

b. Jesus represented himself by actually dying in his own place! We die to ourselves daily, by accepting His sacrifice and choosing to walk in faith.

c. Because He was blameless, He was also able to die in our place, so that we could be in covenant!

d. The covenant? "I will be your Husband, and you will be My Bride!"

e. Before Jesus was crucified, He explained to His disciples what this would look like. He said, *"I am leaving to make a place for you, I am coming back for you, so that you can be with me forever. I have made you pure by my blood (my dying in your place) and I want you to be my beautiful bride. If you accept my sacrifice (drink my blood and eat my body) you will be alive eternally with me,"* (paraphrased from: *John 14:1–6, 1 Corinthians 11:23–26*).

f. Being in covenant with God is about being in such a close relationship with him (like a marriage) that all they He has or possess in this life is available to you upon request, and everything you have is available to Him upon His request!

j. Today, you can choose to be in covenant relationship with God, or if you've already accepted Him as your Lord and Savior (you are already in covenant with Him) you can access the grace you need to live in the purity you want!

k. You may not have what it takes to be sexually pure, but God does! And He is willing to empower you with what He has!

l. In exchange, He can call upon you to share Him with the world around you *(1 Pet 2:9)*!

2. DO YOU KNOW WHERE YOU'RE GOING?

- Purity looks like something. It is reflected in your thoughts and actions.

- What purity looks like in your life, may be different than someone else's

    i. *"I have the right to do anything," you say—but not everything is beneficial. I have the right to do anything"— but not everything is constructive." 2 Cor 10:23 [NIV]*

    ii. God tells us some of the things we may and may not do (eg: [scripture reference]) but others, He wants to teach us on a one-on-one basis.

- You need vision for what you want purity to look like in your life. This is like your goal for purity.

- Without a destination (goal) you won't be very successful in being pure! (Prov 29:18 [VOICE]).

- This looks like saying "NO" to some things (eg: unhealthy relationships, porn, premarital sex, etc.) and saying "YES" to other things (eg: only having sex inside of marriage, giving yourself permission to be yourself, healthy friendships, proper emotional boundaries, protecting your virginity, etc.).

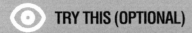

TRY THIS (OPTIONAL)

Lead your group in reading and signing the Purity Covenant (optional)

3. HOW ARE YOU GOING TO GET THERE—PURITY PLAN

- Now that you have VISION and GOALS for your sexual purity, you need a PLAN!

- This plan Includes specific actions you will/will not do that will help you accomplish your goal (what you want)!

- The plan is the action you will take to get what you want.

SHOW THIS

Take a moment to explain the difference between a goal and a plan. Write it on a white board if possible.

PLAN: "I will lose 10 lb," is NOT a plan. It is a GOAL.

GOAL: "I will lose 10 lbs by eating only 1500 calories/day and exercising 30mins/day." IS a plan

PLAN: "My plan is to not lust," is NOT a plan. It is a GOAL.

GOAL: "I will stop lusting by asking God what He thinks about the women I find attractive, and matching my thoughts with His." is a PLAN.

To make an effective plan, ask yourself these three questions

1. *What do I want?*
   (This is your goal. This is what purity will look like.)

2. *What do I need?*
   (This is important to know, so you can DO the right thing.)

3. *What specific action will I take to get it?*
   w(This is your plan. This is what you do.)

4. NEEDS

- As we've learned, we have spirit, soul and body needs, that we are driven to meet. It is often instinctual—we will subconsciously look for ways to get our needs met, if they're not being met.

- We can get our needs met in either an unhealthy or healthy way. Our unhealthy behaviors are often just "US" trying to meet our needs, through an inappropriate source.

- Changing our behaviors won't work unless we *meet the underlying need* that caused us to act out inappropriately to get them met.

- Once you've *identified* what you need, you can DECIDE how you want to meet that need in a healthy way and with God's help, you will be able to DO it!

- It takes time to learn yourself in this way! Be kind to yourself as you learn and grow.

 SHOW THIS

Take a look at the Purity Plan for more on needs and how to meet your needs in a healthy way.

5. ACCOUNTABILITY

- It is important to have people in your life to walk with you on your journey, to encourage you, challenge you and ask you good questions.

- We don't always know what we need or how to get it, so it is important to have people you can go to for wisdom in those areas.

- *Without wise guidance, a nation falls, but victory is certain when there are plenty of wise counselors. (Proverbs 11:14, VOICE)*

- Accountability people could be: a trusted friend, an older couple you know, your parents, etc.

- They will help you talk through and walk out your purity plan. In these relationships you should be able to be gut-honest and vulnerable about your heart and how you're doing in the battle for purity.

- These are people who will help you take ACCOUNT for your ABILITY, not punish you for your disability. They will remind you of your YES, and your vision for sexual purity.

- An accountability partner is NOT someone who struggles with the same thing you do. That wouldn't be helpful! What you really need is someone who is strong and brings you strength.

◉ SHOW THIS (OPTIONAL)

Lead your group in reading and creating their own Purity Plans (optional).

Conclusion: You need all of God to be able to walk in purity—body, soul and spirit! You have been called, redeemed, set apart and empowered to live free of sin, even in your sexuality! God designed you with needs that cause you to be drawn into Him and community (family, friends, church, etc.) to get them met! That's how God made it; you were built for connection with Him and those around you! As we grow and learn what we need and how to get it in a healthy way, we will be setting ourselves up for absolute success in our friendships, dating relationships and marriages. We will be whole, healthy, powerful people who will be able to walk out God's perfect plan for SEX!

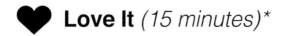 **Love It** *(15 minutes)**

REFLECTION TIME *(Personal)*

- Take some time to think about areas in your life that you have tried to hide or have withheld from God; areas you do not trust the Lord in; areas He is asking you to surrender. Write them down now.

- Have an honest conversation with the Lord about the above areas. Tell Him what you are feeling (afraid, mad, embarrassed, confused, lacking faith, powerless, ashamed, etc.). Invite Him into those areas and, if you are ready, surrender them to Him.

- Reflect on the great price God paid to enter into a covenant relationship with you, Jesus' death on a cross. Do you believe you alone are worth this sacrifice? Take some time to talk to the Lord about these things (optional communion).

CONNECTION QUESTIONS *(Small Group)*

1. Was anything you learned in this lesson about covenant new? surprising? scary? daunting?

2. What is the difference between a covenant and a promise? Explain.

3. Were you aware that you entered into a covenant with God when you accepted Jesus as your savior? How does that change your relationship with Him and the decisions that you make?

4. Are you aware that God views/values your (future) marriage covenant as powerfully as his covenant with you? How does that affect your view of marriage?

5. What is your motivation for entering the purity covenant (should you choose to do so)? Who are you doing it for? (God, yourself, spouse, future children, parents?)

6. Entering a purity covenant will require you to practice a lifestyle of purity. Discuss this statement openly in your small group.

 **Live It** *(15 Minutes)***

MY LIFE

1. Meditate daily on Phil 4:13 which says, "I can do all things through Christ who strengthens me." This week, practice asking the Lord for whatever grace and strength you need throughout the day. Be sure to record/write down your victories this week.

2. This week practice establishing a new and healthy way of thinking/habit in your life. Identify one area that you would like to change and ask the Lord for wisdom and strategies to conquer it. Then go for it!

3. This week, practice a daily habit of thanking/praising the Lord for victories (purity, integrity, love, not going into peer pressure, etc.) in your life—those that you had, those that you are currently going after, and those that are on their way.

MY FRIENDS

1. Choose 3 people to creatively serve in some small way. ie; babysit for free, do a small project around the house, offer free tutoring, do something fun with a younger sibling, wash your coach's car, etc. In this, you will be practicing, sacrifice towards those around you.

2. Find one married couple in your life that you honor and respect and ask them to share their story with you. Ask them for advice in dating/marriage. Ask them to describe what sacrifice looks like to them (within marriage).

3. Get together with a few friends from your youth group and begin to dream/ envision/ write down the kind of marriage you want to have and the kind of legacy you want to leave for your future children.

MY WORLD

1. Is there anyone in my home I have a relational mess with? Do I owe anyone an apology (ask for forgiveness)? Do I need to forgive anyone? Take time this week to make right anything that can be wrong in your home. Own your mistakes; and start new. Remember God resists the proud and gives grace to the humble.

2. Take time this week to reach out, connect and bless your teachers, coaches, and managers. Encourage, pray, and bring your best to them at school, work and extracurricular activities.

3. Ask 2–3 friends in your life for honest feedback about the kind of friend that you are to them. Examples: faithful, honest, dependable, uplifting? Selfish, gossip, rude, critical? Look for opportunities to grow as a friend this week.

Lead It *(5 Minutes)*

1. Any further repentance/restoration needed:

2. Lead your group in signing our Purity Covenant. Read through this agreement as a group. Invite anyone who wishes to either read it again as a declaration, or alternatively, you can print it and invite them to sign their name at the bottom. Consider printing it on 3x5 or 4x8 cards so they can keep them in their Bibles. You may also encourage them to buy purity rings or wristbands as signs of their covenant with God.

3. Walk your group through writing their own purity plans. Send them home to work on, then next week have them share with their small groups/one-on-one time.

AGREEMENTS

Father, I agree that you designed and created my whole being—spirit, soul, and body—including my sexuality, and that You said it was very good. I am powerful, valuable, worthy of Your love, and worthy of an amazing marriage.

I agree that You designed sex, not only as the means of procreation, but as an act of love that establishes a complete spirit, soul, and body bond between a man and a woman. For this reason, sex ought to be expressed solely within the boundaries of a life-long marriage covenant.

I agree that honoring Your guidelines will lead me to Your best for my life.

PLEDGES

I pledge to trust You, my Father, as the One who fulfills my desires. I will look to You as my ultimate source of affection, comfort, happiness, peace, identity, and hope. You are the true love of my life, and I will trust your leading and timing in my life, knowing that You have nothing but the best love story for me to share with you.

I pledge to honor Your design for my sexuality in word, thought, and action. I will steward my physical, emotional, and spiritual desires according to Your guidelines so that they consistently propel me toward you and toward a godly marriage.

I pledge to honor others as fellow sons and daughters of the King, treating them as I wish to be treated, no matter how they treat me. I will think of them with pure thoughts and look at them with pure eyes, as You do. I will not compromise Your standards for my sexuality for anyone, even myself.

I pledge to carry myself as a royal son/daughter whose body, soul, and spirit belong first to You, then to me, and then to the person I marry. I will not give myself sexually, even in my mind and heart, to anyone but my wife/husband.

RECOGNITION

I recognize that You have made every provision for me to manage my sex drive well and become fully prepared to experience sex and marriage as You designed them. I can do all things through Christ's strength *(see Phil. 4:13).*

I recognize that You have promised to fulfill the desires of my heart as I delight in You *(see Ps. 37:4)*, including my desires for sex and marriage.

I recognize that You have promised to provide a way of escape from every temptation *(see 1 Cor. 10:13).*

I recognize that You have promised to fully forgive and restore me after every failure. You invite me to come before You boldly when I need Your mercy and grace *(see Heb. 4:16).*

I recognize that You are always with me, that nothing can separate me from Your love, that I hear Your voice, that I am fully accepted by You no matter what I do, and that You always delight in me.

PASTOR LETTER

Dear Pastor,

We wanted to let you know that we have recently purchased a copy of a 6-week course entitled, "Let's Talk About It: Sexuality" and would very much like to run this in the church youth group. It has been written by an organization called Moral Revolution, who produce resources designed to equip and empower society to wholeness.

They seek to address the root causes of purity issues rather than just communicate the message: "abstain from having sex" and also to call people to a higher standard of living, imparting value for the heart and encouraging them to walk in all that God has created them to be.

We believe the church should be the safest, most empowering environment when it comes to modeling what love looks like and be the best at helping people learn how to manage their God-given sex drive. It was with this in mind that we considered their material a great option to teach our youth, and make it our goal to begin discussing and releasing freedom regarding these "shamed" topics; putting them into the context of a kingdom perspective.

However, before we ran ahead with the idea we wanted to submit it to you as our overseeing Pastor(s) and allow you to review the course content, as we are aware that some of it is sensitive and frank in nature. The course views purity as a lifestyle of holiness—being separate from anything that debases, contaminates or pollutes our body, soul or spirit. It builds a biblical perspective on a number of subjects, including (but not limited to): identity, the nature of God, the purpose of sex, our needs, the effects of sexual behavior in our body, soul and spirit, and building a vision for sexual purity that will carry an individual through their single years, into marriage and beyond.

We would love to have your endorsement as we forge ahead to lead this course.

Much Grace,

If you would also like to look into more of who Moral Revolution are then feel free to browse their website, www.moralrevolution.com for further information.

PARENT LETTER

Dear Parents,

We are excited to announce that we are starting a six week series on purity, wholeness, and sex called "Let's Talk About It: SEXUALITY" by Moral Revolution. In these upcoming weeks, we will be discovering and discussing Heaven's blueprints for sex and sexuality so that we can build healthy individuals, relationships, and futures... the way God designed them to be!

Purity is not just abstinence. Purity is a lifestyle of holiness: being separate from anything that debases, contaminates, or pollutes our bodies, souls, or spirits. Looking at purity in this holistic way, we are embarking on a journey to build a Biblical perspective on sex. We'll cover a number of foundational principles, including (but not limited to): identity, the nature of God, the purpose of sex, needs, the effects of sexual behaviors in our our bodies, souls, or spirits, and building a vision for sexual purity that will carry them through their single years into marriage and beyond!

Because we understand that some of our content is sensitive in nature, we'd like to invite you to look over the six week summary we've attached and prayerfully consider which sessions you'd like your child to participate in or if you'd like more information on one or more of our lessons. We believe that it is important for you to be the loudest voice in your child's life regarding sex, so, if there is any way we can support you in that, please don't hesitate to contact us!

Thank you for honoring us with your trust and the privilege of walking with your child on this leg of their journey with the Lord. We value your prayers! Continue to pray that this series will impact our students, empowering them to live boldly in the freedom and purity that Jesus paid for!

PURITY COVENANT

A covenant is a binding promise made between two people. This kind of promise ties you together with another person. Each person is responsible to fulfill what they have agreed to in the promise. Each person brings their strength to the relationship to make sure the promise is kept. These people are in such close relationship with each other that all they have or possess in this life is available to each other upon request. In Bible times, this kind of promise could only be dissolved if one of the covenanters died. It is a life-long promise that binds you together for one common purpose.

In making a purity covenant, you are making a promise to both yourself and to God. You are in it for life—it can only end if one of you dies! The purpose? For you to be able to live whole and healthy in your sexuality, both now and after you're married. God wants you to be entirely yourself, the way He created you to be—body, soul, and spirit—knowing that this will enable you to fully enjoy an intimate marital relationship with the man or woman of your dreams. He is fully supportive of you and promises never to leave you or forsake you in your journey, and He will give you His strength where you are weak. He asks you to choose to run after purity and to trust Him, that He is protecting you and leading you into His love story for your life.

The love story that God has for you is not just a story, but your own real-life experience with Him—living in love with God. That is what we are inviting you to grab onto for yourself. That is the biggest "yes" you can ever make. You can say "yes" for other reasons, and that might get you down the purity highway for a while, but ultimately, you need God's comfort, love and grace to be able to live the life that's in your heart to live.

In order for you to one day love your spouse, you must first love yourself. The Bible is clear that we love others in the way we love ourselves (Matthew 22:39). In making a purity covenant with yourself, you are promising yourself that you will love, honor, and cherish the way you were made, including your sexuality. After all that we have learned about our design as human beings, it is easy to see that one of the best ways to love yourself and experience sex in its fullness, is to guard your heart and keep sex for marriage.

In saying yes to the things listed below, understand that you are inherently saying NO to other things. There is only so much room in your life, and you get to choose what will be there. Replace the bad with good, and the bad will not have room to stay. So, instead of making this a promise about the things you say NO to, it will be covenant about (a YES to) doing the right things. What you focus on, you make room for in your life; keep your eyes focused on the goal, and you'll become a winner!

In signing this covenant I, _____ am saying YES to:

a) My value as a son or daughter of God. I will freely receive God's love, affirmation, and correction.

b) Having people in my life (eg. fathers, mothers, leaders etc) who can speak into my decisions and help me live the best life I can choose for myself.

c) Valuing my whole being by only having a sexual relationship with my spouse (future or current).

d) Staying honest and connected with my heart (emotions, thoughts, and feelings) while in my process.

e) Protecting myself by being careful about what I look at, think about, and touch.

f) Protecting others by my words and actions, in what I say, how I view them, how I behave towards them.

g) Being powerful and assertive in taking care of my needs in a healthy way.

h) Cultivating and celebrating my unique masculinity/femininity to honor my design as a man/woman.

i) Transparency and vulnerability. I will allow people to see me and allow myself to be known.

j) A life of integrity. I will be a person who does what I say I will do.

k) Not hiding who I am, but allowing who I am on the inside to manifest on the outside.

l) Dressing and behaving in a way that reflects who I am on the inside.

m) Respecting myself and my boyfriend/girlfriend in our mutual pursuit of each other.

n) Allowing God to meet my needs for intimacy, connection and comfort, before getting them met from a counterfeit source.

o) _____

p) _____

q) _____

While the most important YES is said first in your heart, it is important to share your choice with others. Below is a space to sign your YES. This will be a reminder to you of your brave choice and it will allow others to be a part of your process, to walk with you and celebrate every victory you have on your journey!

COVENANT

I _____, make a this Covenant of Purity

with myself and God on _____.

WITNESSES

(People who will walk with you and help you stay accountable to your YES.)

X_____

X_____

X_____

PURITY PLAN

INTRO

If you fail to plan, you are planning to fail. Many of us have had excellent, pure intentions and have wholeheartedly chosen to live a pure life, to save ourselves for marriage, and to have honorable relationships; yet, many of us don't. Why? It is because we don't have a map that shows us how to get there.

Making your own purity plan will give you practical steps to walking in purity toward your ultimate goals: a healthy marriage, exciting, pure, passionate sex with the person of your dreams, and a healthy YOU for the rest of your life.

Your purity plan will be unique to you. Not everyone has the same struggles or weaknesses. Much in the same way that not everyone likes the same foods, movies, or hairstyles, not everyone will be attracted to or turned on by the same things. Because of this, it's important for YOU to understand yourself and what you're attracted to or tempted by. Remember, you're not looking at your weaknesses to punish yourself for failure, but instead, are shining light on potholes and pits that you want to avoid as you make your way down the purity highway. By being honest with yourself, you'll be able to remain powerful and in control of yourself, as you grow in intimacy in your relationships.

God clearly draws SOME of the boundary lines for us in scripture, ie: no sex outside of marriage, no sex with someone who is not your spouse, do not lust. However, other things He wants to discuss with you on a one-on-one basis.

Your purity plan is in place to help you decide where and how to draw your personal boundary lines. This will include what you will and will not do or allow in your life: what things you will look at, think about, and touch. Discussed below are some ideas that everyone should take into account when considering what it will take for them to live a pure life, especially in their sexuality.

PART 1: GETTING OUR NEEDS MET

Most of the time, we struggle with our sexual purity because we have not taken care of our internal needs for intimacy, connection, comfort, identity, purpose, etc. Remember: Once you've taken care of your spirit and soul needs, your physical needs quiet down. Your sex drive becomes manageable when you've met your needs in a proper, healthy way. As you do this, your spirit's "voice" becomes louder than your body's desires. It becomes easier to say no to the things you don't want to do, and easier to do the things you do want to do. We are not saying "no" to our body's real, healthy needs, but learning to function in the way we were created to.

With that in mind, let's talk about making a purity plan to get your spirit and soul needs met.

A) Connection with God

You are a spirit being created for connection with God through His Holy Spirit. When your spirit is connected to God's Spirit, He is able to meet your needs for identity and purpose as well as supply you with intimacy, connection, and comfort. For example, if you struggle with feelings of insecurity, loneliness, the need to distract yourself through work, hobbies, or relationships (ie: you're afraid to be alone with yourself), you may need to focus on your spiritual connection with God.

Some ways you can do this are:

1. Make the decision to be in relationship with God. Accept the sacrifice Jesus has made for you, realizing that you have been forgiven for anything and everything that you have ever done wrong or failed to do. Allow Him to be the Lord of your life, and commit to being in relationship with Him, which means allowing Him to dwell within you, lead you, and guide you in every circumstance of your life.

2. Connect with God DAILY. You need to make sure your spirit is well fed. We all have different ways we feel connected to God and different ways we hear His voice. Some things you can do to connect with Him may be: reading the Bible, prayer, worship, enjoying nature, doing things you like and find refreshing, or simply acknowledging He is constantly with you.

3) In crisis moments or when you have failed, run TO God, not FROM Him. Always be quick to talk to Him about your problem, and allow yourself to receive forgiveness and grace to do it better the next time. Talk to Him about your pain, frustration, anger, disappointment, etc. Don't hide anything from Him. Be very honest with Him. He already knows what you're going through, He's not surprised and He has the answers you need.

Trust God from the bottom of your heart; don't try to figure out everything on your own. Listen for God's voice in everything you do, everywhere you go; he's the one who will keep you on track."
Proverbs 3:5–6 (MSG)

B) Connection With Yourself

When it comes to making a purity plan, we often try to modify our behaviors from the wrong ones to the right ones. That's hard to do when you don't know WHY you're doing the wrong thing. As we've discussed, you're not doing the wrong thing just because you're bad. You're doing it because you're trying to get a need met in the wrong way. Like trying to fuel a car with water, you won't get very far by filling your needs with the wrong "fuel." So, the goal is, to find out WHAT YOU NEED.

Find Out What You Need.

Some of our needs are obvious; we need proper sleep, to eat well, air to breathe, a safe place to live, etc. Having these very basic needs met will dramatically affect the choices we make. For example, can you remember a time where you were so hungry or tired that you were outrageously grumpy, or even violent? Did you just brush it off saying, "I'm just tired," or "I'm just hungry?" When your stomach rumbles, you know you feel hungry, you need FOOD. When your eyes are droopy and you feel sleepy you need REST. Easy, right?

Other needs are not always so easy to identify. They sometimes elude us because we ignore our feelings, which are meant to act like the lights on a car dashboard. When an emotion pops up, it's to help us identify what is going on inside of us. When we know what is going on inside of us, we can help ourselves get what we need. (Eg: You are anxious: Are you feeling afraid? Tired? Hurt? Hungry? If you are feeling hungry, and are anxious due to low blood sugar, you can get food. If you are hurt, you can work on resolving the conflict, or getting encouragement. If you feel tired, you can go take a nap. If you feel afraid, you can get yourself into safety, or receive comfort from God, a friend, or family member!) If we can begin to recognize and name our feelings, we will have won half the battle in getting our needs met.

We all need love, affection and attention, comfort, connection, intimacy, and purpose, among other things! We can get our needs met spiritually, emotionally, and physically. Many of us learned that "all we need is God." But that is not entirely accurate. It is true that all good gifts come from God, He is the Creator and ultimately our sustainer, but we were made by God with the capacity for relationship, and our capacity needs to be used. It is in our design! God intended for us to get some of our needs met through relationship with other people! For example, babies who are not touched will die. If God could meet all of their needs, that wouldn't be so. It is no different with children, teenagers, or adults: we need other people in order to get some of our needs met. God needs a body to work through—you, me, and those around us.

If you're struggling with sexual behaviors, it is very likely that some of your needs are not getting met. Knowing it or not, you are probably finding a way to quench the feeling of your need, without meeting it properly. Fear not, you will be able to discover WHY you did what you did, and you can use those bad experiences to your advantage.

To practice this, we are going to learn to identify your red flags (feelings or behaviors that occur before you make a poor choice) and your triggers (what circumstances/experience lit your fuse, starting the process of the poor choice). First, think of a time that you made a poor choice. Think about what you were doing, thinking, or feeling before you made a mistake and did the thing you didn't want to do. The feelings or thoughts, or (possibly) behaviors are your red flags. They should act like neon red flags, highlighting that something isn't right: you need something in that moment! What you were doing, where you were, what was happening, could be your triggers. The stressful moment, the new environment, the insult, etc. could all be things that you reacted to negatively. We call them your triggers because they "set you off," starting a chain reaction, like a bomb going off! If you can see your red flags, or understand that your fuse has been lit, you can put it out, or meet the need intentionally, in a healthy way.

Example 1: *A young man goes home for Christmas with his family. He has never felt wanted in his parents house. Like every holiday, he got in a fight with his dad and started yelling, then shut down and wouldn't talk to anyone all afternoon. He brooded over the argument for a while, then stuffed it down saying, "Whatever. He's just a jerk...". Later that evening, he meets up with his girlfriend and finds himself pressing her to go too far, physically. The next day, he avoids his dad, feeling numb.*

Q: What would he say his problem is?
A: Going too far with his girlfriend.

Q: What was his real problem?
A: Disconnection from and conflict with his dad. Not feeling loved by his parents.

Q: Why did he act out with his girlfriend?
A: Being intimate with her made him feel powerful, and loved, meeting his needs.

Q: What were his red flags?
A: Anger, yelling, shutting down emotionally.

Q: What were his triggers?
A: His dad yelling at him. Being in an unsafe place.

Q: What was he feeling?
A: Powerless, angry, hurt, sad, disrespected.

Q: What did he need?
A: Comfort, affirmation, to feel powerful.

Q: How could he have met his need in a healthy way?
A: He could have called a friend to talk out his feelings of frustration and pain at (once again) fighting with his dad, and/or never feeling welcome at his parent's home. He could have allowed himself time to really feel and understand the pain and frustration, instead of bottling it all up, then letting himself process it (get it out) by talking to God, boxing, running, and journalling. He could have found one family member whom he got along with well to spend some time with. He could have left.

Example 2: *A girl walks into a bar...seriously. On her 21st birthday, her family celebrated her. Kind of. There was a nice card waiting for her and a cake after dinner, but there were no hugs and no sentimental words. But she tried to ignore her disappointment, after all, that wasn't strange, her family was never affectionate. After dinner, her friends took her out to the bar, just for fun. A guy approached her, and offered to buy her a drink. She blushed and accepted. Over the course of their conversation, she began spilling her heart, sharing things with him that she had never told anyone else. One thing led to another and the next morning, she woke up in his bed.*

Q: What would she say her problem is?
A: She's a slut. She sleeps with random people.

Q: What was her real problem?
A: She did not receive the love and affirmation she needed from her family.

Q: Why did she go home with the guy?
A: His attention made her feel powerful, seen, valued, wanted.

Q: What were her red flags?
A: An unusual, close connection with a stranger. (Not normal!) Feeling of desperately wanting him, followed by fear of rejection.

Q: What were her triggers?
A: Not feeling special on her birthday. Being in a new place with no boundaries, a place where she felt free.

Q: What was she feeling?
A: Hidden, unloved, unvalued, unimportant.

Q: What did she need?
A: To feel known, heard, seen, celebrated. Healthy affectionate touch. Affirmation of her value.

Q: How could she have met her need in a healthy way?
A: She could have had her girl friends join her family for dinner. They could have done her favorite things, to help her feel known, seen, celebrated, etc. She could pray and journalabout her feelings and ask God to show her who He says she is, and how crazily HE celebrates her. She could talk to her parents and share with them what makes her feel loved, so they could better show her love in a way that makes her feel loved.

Ask yourself: What is it that happens on your "bad days?" Why were you feeling/thinking what you were? What were you feeling? Were you: Hurt? Angry? Lonely? Tired? Were you feeling rejected and needed comfort? Were you feeling lonely and needed connection? Were you feeling scared and needed to feel powerful again? Were you feeling numb and needed intimacy? Were you feeling depressed because you needed to feel loved? Once you can identify the need, you can employ your will, choosing to meet it in the right way.

2) Brainstorm How to Meet Your Needs. You may be able to do some of this on your own, but discussing it with those you trust can give you valuable insights. They may help you find answers you couldn't have come up with on your own. [SEE: Part 2, Accountability] If you have no one to talk to right now, you can start by asking God for His wisdom, then asking yourself good questions like: What makes me feel comforted? Talking with a friend? Hanging out with a parent? Getting a good grade on an assignment? Having a nap? Then ask yourself, "Is that a healthy way to get my need for comfort met?" Knowing yourself in this way is a process, so be kind to yourself as you learn.

3) Set Boundaries for Success. Once you've discovered what you need and have a plan to meet those needs, you can set yourself up for success by guarding your weak areas.

For example: A person knows that when he feels lonely and tired, he needs to be comforted. Normally, he would try to distract himself from those feelings by getting on the Internet, which leaves him vulnerable to using pornography because it gives him the feeling of being connected and intimate, if only just for a moment. What could his boundary be? How could he protect his weak area? He could choose to not get on the computer when he knows he feels lonely or tired. Instead, when he realizes he feels lonely and tired, he chooses to call a friend/family member or write in his journal before going to sleep. This helps him to work through his feelings and receive comfort instead of avoiding them.

In your life, your boundaries could include: your bedtime, what time you take your date home, what movies you watch, if you'll close your bedroom door, whom you have close relationships with, when you will/won't get on the Internet, etc.

Without wise guidance, a nation falls, but victory is certain when there are plenty of wise counselors. *Proverbs 11:14 (VOICE)*

PART 2: BOUNDARIES IN RELATIONSHIPS

A) Where's The Line?

The question you're probably wondering is: Where's "the line?" How far can I go with my boyfriend/girlfriend physically? Is it okay to kiss? What about oral sex? What can I do and still be pure?

The Bible is clear that any kind of sex (including oral and anal) before or outside of marriage is not okay. However, the Bible does not clearly draw "the line" for physical contact. This is something you need to decide for yourself, with God and wise counsel based on what your personal turn-ons are. Scientifically, we know that your body begins the process of sex at arousal. Because of this, we recommend that you know what arouses you, and choose to refrain from behaviors that turn you on.

B) Know Your Turn-On's

It is important to consider what things turn you on, both physical and nonphysical. This will help you choose how you will behave around and toward your significant other. Again, by avoiding behaviors that arouse either of you, you are protecting your hearts and your relationship. It is also an opportunity to learn how to work together as a team to take care of each other.

You and your significant other may have different opinions on what is "okay" and what is not. This will depend on 1) your convictions and 2) your turn-ons. You need to respect each other's boundaries. If one of you is not okay with kissing, neither of you will be kissing. If one of you is not okay with cuddling, there will be no cuddling. Have honest conversations with each other about your turn-ons. In doing this, you'll learn how to show each other love, honor, and respect on this side of your vows.

What turns you on? Kissing? Cuddling? Holding hands? Imagining them naked? Fantasizing about your relationship? Seeing your significant other in a bathing suit? It might sound funny to think about, but if you can leave the things that arouse you for after your wedding vows, you will build trust, understanding and emotional intimacy. You will have a strong, healthy relationship, free from frustration and baggage.

C) Strengthen Your Weak Areas

Again, assess your (potential) weak areas: Are you staying up too late together, putting yourselves in situations where you can't make good decisions? When you are unable to feel connected or go deeper with each other, do you try to use your physical relationship to go deeper? Are you connecting too intimately too quickly? Has your relationship drawn you away from friends and community?

If you're prone to making mistakes in your physical relationship, take some time to assess your behaviors. What habits, choices, or circumstances leave you vulnerable to making mistakes? Are you trying to meet your needs in an unhealthy way? Once you've discovered what you need, make a plan to meet those needs and draw boundaries that will protect your weak areas. You may choose to: set a curfew, spend more time (together) with friends, date in public places, change your physical boundaries, etc.

D) Accountability

You need help. Just like you needed others to help you as an infant, you cannot supply yourself with everything you need as you begin to grow in your journey to purity. You need people in your life who are going to love you, ask you good questions, encourage you, and remind you of what you want and how you've chosen to get there. We would call these people in your life your "accountability." They could be a trusted friend, an older couple you know, or your parents. These people are there to help you talk through and walk out your purity plan. In these relationships, you should be able to be gut-honest and vulnerable about your heart and how you're doing in the battle for purity. These are people who will help you take ACCOUNT for your ABILITY, not punish you for your inability to do it on our own. They will remind you of your YES.

Accountability relationships are safe and trustworthy relationships that should have the following characteristics:

1. They understand that you are on a learning journey. They do not expect perfection and they are extremely patient in helping you move forward, even when you stumble.

2. They won't disrespect you by taking control of your life in any way or telling you what they think. They will simply offer what they know from their own experience and ask questions that help you better think for yourself.

3. They will respect your relationship with the Holy Spirit and their guidance will lead you toward deeper intimacy and trust with Him.

4. They will treat you like a prince/princess who is destined and able to become a powerful and pure lover of God.

5. They speak about sex with honor and without shame. You should feel safe and invited to bring up any sexual questions or concerns that you have.

6. They will be passionate and uncompromising about God's standards for your life. They will be unafraid to confront you, in love, with God's standard.

7. They should be free of any bondage you're dealing with. An accountability partner is not someone who struggles with the same thing you do. That wouldn't be helpful! What you really need is someone who is strong and brings you strength.

If you are in a relationship, it is a good idea for the two of you to meet with this person/couple to help you chart the course of your relationship and encourage and strengthen you as you manage your sexual desires before (and even after) marriage. These people should never be responsible to control or police you both as you protect your purity. It is your responsibility to pursue and invite open communication about how you're managing yourselves. This may seem scary, but the strength and wisdom someone offers you could help you live free of guilt and shame.

If your significant other does not share your boundaries and is not willing to respect them, your boundaries and accountability will not work. You cannot pull someone into purity. You cannot change their heart by trying to control their actions. If they want to do the opposite of you, there is nothing you can do to change that. If that sounds like your relationship, the first step in your purity plan may be to break up. Your boundaries control YOU, not other people. You make your choices. They make theirs. That may sound harsh, but in the long run, it is better to set yourself up for success by finding someone who will work with you for purity, instead of against you.

"I charge you not to excite your love until it is ready.
Don't stir a fire in your heart too soon, until it is ready to be satisfied."

Song of Solomon 8:4 (VOICE)

"Live in true devotion to one another, loving each other as sisters and brothers. Be first to honor others by putting them first."

Romans 12:10 (VOICE)

PART 3: MY PURITY PLAN

What's your plan? If your plan sounds something like, "My plan is to lose 10 lbs." "My plan is to be famous." "My plan is to not masturbate," you need to know that you do not have a plan.

What you will or will not do may be part of your plan, but it is not a plan. For example, the statement, "I will not look at pornography," is a GOAL not a PLAN. The goal is the outcome you want. The plan is the action you will take to get what you want. The statement, "I will stop lusting by asking God what He thinks about the women I find attractive," is a PLAN. Your GOAL may be included in your plan, but you need to have an action you will DO to get your goal.

Once you have some goals and some plans to meet your goals, share your plan with someone you are accountable to—perhaps the people who witnessed and signed your Purity Covenant— and get some feedback. Make a plan to connect with them on a set date, about once a month, if not more often. If either of you cannot commit to that, perhaps you need to find a different accountability—you need to be able to have access to them, and talking with them once every three months probably won't be enough! If you have a boyfriend/girlfriend, you will want to talk about your physical relationship and boundaries and make a plan for the two of you. Share this with your accountability person/ couple. This will show them what standard you've chosen for yourself and how they can help you on your journey.

Remember: you are made of a spirit, soul, and body, so make sure you include something for each of those parts of you in your plan! The more specific you can be in your actions, the better. Your plan is somewhat fluid, and may change over time. This is your own personal roadmap: yours will be unique to you! Test drive your plan—if it doesn't work, or have the effect you were hoping for, change it! You may not be meeting your needs correctly, or you may have unrealistic expectations on yourself. This is a work in progress, it will change and grow as you do!

While making your plan, ask yourself these questions:

- What are my "red-flags" and/or triggers?
- What are you feeling, thinking about or experiencing BEFORE you made an unhealthy choice? What was going on? This will help you identify what you were feeling, and why you were feeling it.
- What am I feeling?
- Identify what you're feeling. Eg: Angry? Powerless? Inadequate? Lonely? Misunderstood? This will help highlight what you need.
- What do I need?
- Identify in the moment what you need. What were you trying to get? This is important to know so you can DO the right thing. Eg: Power? Validation? Comfort? Intimacy? Encouragement? Sleep?
- What am I going to do about it?
- What specific action will I take to get my need met, in a healthy way (from the right source)? This is your plan. This is what you do.

Here are some fill-in-the blank examples to help you start writing your purity plan:

"Because of my need for _____ I am going to _____."

"When I feel _____, I will _____."

"I will break the habit of _____ by _____."

MY PURITY PLAN

NAME _____ DATE _____

SPIRIT

Examples:

1. Because of my need for confidence (identity, affirmation, etc.) I will read my Bible daily to learn what God says about me.

2. Because I know that I usually look to a person, activity, or thing to bring me identity, I will ask the Holy Spirit to prompt me when this is happening.

3. I will make declarations at least once a week about my identity.

4. I will forgive my dad for being harsh and critical, and invite God to give me the love/affirmation I need from a Father.

5. When I make a mistake, I will not punish myself, but will repent and forgive myself. I will use that opportunity to discover more about my needs. and think about what it was that I needed at that time.

Write your own:

1.

2.

3.

4.

5.

SOUL *(Mind, Will, Emotions)*

Examples:

1. (Girl) I will break the habit of going to guys with all my problems by choosing to call my female friends when I'm upset.
2. When I feel depressed, low, or hopeless, I will talk to God and journal about my feelings. If I need it, I will then call a friend/family member and connect with them.
3. I will not talk on the phone/text/chat with the opposite sex after 10pm.
4. Because I need to feel important, I will share my accomplishments and victories with my best friend: (name here).
5. I will break the habit of looking at pornography by allowing myself to think about and feel my emotions. I will not try to distract myself when I'm hurting, but instead I will let myself cry.

Write your own:

1.

2.

3.

4.

5.

BODY *(Physical)*

Examples:

1. I will take care of my body, including my mind and emotions, by eating healthy food and getting 8 hours of sleep every night.
2. Because I don't think straight when I'm tired, I will go to sleep instead of watching late night TV.
3. I will not drink alcohol when I'm out on a date, because it impairs my judgment.
4. My girlfriend/boyfriend and I will not kiss on the lips until we are engaged.
5. I will wear modest clothing that reflects who I am on the inside.

Write your own:

1.

2.

3.

4.

5.

FREQUENTLY ASKED QUESTIONS

TEACHER'S GUIDE

This Question and Answer section can be used in two ways. It can be used as reference material for you, the teacher, to provide you with answers to tough questions before one-on-ones, group discussions, or teaching from the front. It can also be used directly in teaching (ie: you read the answers straight from the paper). For easy reading and comprehension, we have chosen to answer questions in the first person. This will allow you to use the content as though it was your own thought.

Masturbation

Q. *What does the Bible say about masturbation? Is it a sin?*

A. The Bible speaks of purity, holiness, and sexuality in many different ways, but never masturbation directly. However, this does not mean that we are giving you permission to masturbate. The real issue is that masturbation entails lusting after people, images and/or creates a fantasy world. In Matthew 5:28, lusting after someone is described as committing adultery. What you orgasm to, you bond to. Your body and brain create memories around the orgasm, and that is why it becomes so addicting. 1 Thessalonians 4:3–8 tells us that we should avoid sexual immorality and that we need to learn to control our own bodies. We are called to be pure and live a holy life.

We have been given a lot of freedom in Christ but that doesn't mean everything we can do is good. I would encourage you to discuss this with a trustworthy leader, or friend of your same sex and get his or her feedback. I would also invite you to have them keep you accountable in this area.

Make sure to take the time to educate yourself, read through some resources, take it before God and make a decision based on truths and your own personal conviction. God gave us free will. It is our job to manage it well. He will speak to you. He will direct you.

Q. *I have tried to stop masturbating, but it seems like I fail every time. How can I have victory over this?*

A. Often times, we think that we can just say a simple prayer and then our problem or habit will disappear. The Lord can fully answer your prayer and help walk you through living a pure and holy life, but we also need to have a plan. First of all, you need to recognize what the root issue is, or if you are fulfilling a need. Are you feeling lonely, tired, stressed, insufficient or upset? Are you not getting your needs met spiritually, emotionally or physically? Begin to figure out what is triggering you to masturbate. Think back to the times you masturbated and look to see what you were doing beforehand. Were you watching a show that has sexual innuendos? Were you feeling bored or listening to music that has sexual content? Once you recognize what is leading you to masturbate you need to go to the Lord, and invite him to fulfill the places of your life where you are lacking intimacy. Don't be afraid to ask Him for self control and a greater ability to manage yourself.

I would encourage you to get some good accountability in your life. This means have two or three people of your same sex you can call at any time to tell them you are struggling with wanting to masturbate, or that you just masturbated. Find safe people that you trust that can be there to pray for you or give you some practical tools on what to do. The best thing you can do to ensure that masturbation is no longer going to be an issue for you, is to stay in community! Share all of who you are with those people you trust and don't be afraid to tell them you are struggling. One of the meanings of intimacy is "into me you see". Let God see you and let other people see you. Often times we feel alone in an issue like this, but there are many people who have this issue or that have overcome it.

Don't give up! The Lord has so much grace to extend to you in this issue, and He will forgive you every time you mess up. Be careful not to let shame and guilt keep you from the Father and from others. Don't keep this problem in the dark because once it is brought to the light it loses its power over you. As long as you are fighting, you are winning.

Refer to these scriptures

1 Corinthians 6:12 (NIV) "I have the right to do anything," you say—but not everything is beneficial. "I have the right to do anything"—but I will not be mastered by anything.

Romans 12:2 (NIV) Do not conform to the pattern of this world, but be transformed by the renewing of your mind. Then you will be able to test and approve what God's will is—his good, pleasing and perfect will.

Sex

Q. *Are oral and anal sex considered sex? Are they okay in a dating relationship? Why or why not?*

A. One of the definitions of sex is any type of sexual activity; this includes anal and oral sex. Anytime there are bodily fluids, genitals and naked bodies involved, it is sex. It is a part of foreplay and plays a major role in your sex life. It takes you to a place of intimacy in your dating relationship that does not match up with your level of commitment. Any kind of sex is made for a husband and wife inside of covenant.

If you are having oral sex or anal sex with someone you are dating, you are creating unhealthy soul ties. In the event of a break up from that person it is going to be a lot more painful for you. If you have already done this with someone, I would encourage you to first of all be kind and gracious with yourself, and seek out some help. Meet with someone who can walk you through the inner healing process and break off soul ties that were formed. Start new, forgive yourself, and begin to receive God's forgiveness. In the previous lessons we shared a purity plan you can use to develop yours.

Q. *I think about sex all of the time, is that normal?*

A. Yes you are completely normal! Thinking about sex is a part of having a sex drive. It is what you do with these thoughts that matters. Learning how to manage your sexual thoughts is a huge part of purity. Being in control of your thoughts and feelings towards sex is key. Remember we become what we behold. We need to be aware of the truths that we agree with. If you agree that you're a powerful person with strong self control, you'll become that person. I would encourage you to talk to someone about your thought life, and have them hold you accountable. Also, ask the Lord to refresh and renew your mind. The Father is so ready and willing to help you through this process!

Q. *What are the effects of sex before marriage?*

A. First of all, God created sex to be powerful. This means having sex outside of marriage is still powerful. However, just because something is powerful does not mean it's always good when it is outside of what God intended.

Sex outside of marriage can have major physical consequences. Things such as STD's (sexually transmitted diseases) and early pregnancy are just a couple of the repercussions you need to think about before you choose to have sex. Statistics show that young girls can be more prone to cancer of the uterus later on in life from having sex too early.

The emotional consequences are that sex is a bonding act and you'll always feel bonded to that person in an unhealthy way. Sex is not only a physical act, you're involving your body, soul and spirit and that's why there is such a strong bond. It is also very common to have feelings of shame, guilt and remorse.

If you have had sex outside of marriage, we have a faithful God that makes all things new. He is able to restore your virginity, and bring healing to your body, emotions and spirit. There are countless stories about women and men that felt like their virginity was completely whole again on their wedding day. And He is able give you a great sex life with your future spouse.

Refer to these scriptures
Ephesians 4:22–24 (NIV) You were taught, with regard to your former way of life, to put off your old self, which is being corrupted by its deceitful desires; to be made new in the attitude of your minds; and to put on the new self, created to be like God in true righteousness.

Galatians 5:19 (NIV) The acts of the flesh are obvious: sexual immorality, impurity and debauchery; idolatry and witchcraft; hatred, discord, jealousy, fits of rage, selfish ambition, dissensions, factions and envy; drunkenness, orgies, and the like. I warn you, as I did before, that those who live like this will not inherit the kingdom of God.

Same Sex Attraction

Q. *I am a girl attracted to other girls, what do I do about that? Does that mean I am gay?*

A. Firstly, I want to say that your identity is not based on your sexual attraction. Just because you feel attracted to the same sex does not mean that you are "gay". It means that you are human and you have a sex drive. Whether you are a girl attracted to a guy, or a girl attracted to a girl, you still have to manage your sexual feelings. Just because you have sexual feelings towards the same sex, does not mean you need to act on them. Many times it can feel like you are the only one feeling this way, and it can be easy for you to isolate yourself and feel alone. I want to tell you that you are not alone in this. You just have a need for intimacy which is how God designed you. Intimacy is feeling known and being known by people who love you.

Sometimes we mix up intimacy with sexual attraction because the only intimacy we have been told about and know is sexual. Sex and intimacy are not the same thing and it is possible to have intimacy without having sex. You were created by God to have a need for intimacy which at its simplest state is a strong connection and familiarity within friendships. We were made for intimacy with other men and women and having healthy female friendships, is very important. I would encourage you to seek out relationships with people who you feel safe with and can really know and love you. Most importantly seek out a deep intimate relationship with God and see what He has to say about you and who you are as a woman.

There are so many reasons why you could be feeling attracted to the same sex. Many times when someone is molested at a young age by the same sex, it can create a false view of what love looks like. This may lead you to view other women sexually because all you've been taught is that sexual acts are between two women. Then you have the other side of this. Some women who have been raped or taken advantage of by men, no longer feel like they can trust them. This can cause a girl to think she needs to be with a girl because they feel safer.

Another reason you could be feeling this way is you may have been labeled as "gay" by some of your peers. The world has this view that athletic girls are "butch" and therefore "lesbian". I want to tell you that this is a lie. Just because you don't like to wear makeup or wear dresses does not make you any less of a woman. We are all so unique and the world needs what you have to offer. When we start to believe a lie like this, it becomes who we are. When we are constantly called something or told something that is not true about us, we begin to agree with the lie. As soon as you agree with the lie, it starts to have control over you. The bible says that life and death are in the power of the tongue, which makes declarations so powerful. Begin to declare life and love over yourself. Speak truth and hope over yourself as well.

Are you simply just needing healthy love and affection from the same sex? Are you needing a healthy mother to come into your life? There could be many different reasons why you are reverting to this.

There has also been a lie that we need to "experiment" with our sexuality and find out what works for us. The world says that it is okay to be curious with the opposite sex and test it out. This is not true. The enemy would love nothing more than to tell you lies like this, but God created sex to be between a man and a woman. This needs to become a reality in your life. Begin to hang out with healthy married couples and watch how they interact with one another.

Most importantly, be kind to yourself. We are all human and we all have things we are working through. Extend grace to yourself and allow yourself to process through this with the Lord. He is gracious and compassionate with us, allow Him to invade the deepest parts of your heart and invite Him into your mess. He wants to help you get free, and be all He created you to be!

Q. *I am a guy attracted to other guys, what do I do about that? Does that mean I'm gay?*

A. Firstly, I want to say that your identity is not your sexual attraction. Just because you feel attracted to the same sex does not mean that you are "gay". It means that you are human and you have a sex drive. Whether you are a guy attracted to a girl, or a guy attracted to a guy, you still have to manage your sexual feelings. Just because you have sexual feelings towards the same sex, does not mean you need to act on them. Many times it can feel like you are the only one feeling this way, and it can be easy for you to isolate yourself and feel very alone. I want to tell you that you are not alone in this.

Secondly, I think it is important to clarify that having emotions as well as feelings, and being sensitive does not mean you are any less of a man. Also if you're extremely creative and artistic doesn't mean your are more effeminate. The world has painted this picture of a man being muscular, fearless, independent and disconnected from their emotions. However, the most healthy manly man in the world was Jesus; who was often found weeping, caring for others and moved with compassion as He interacted with friends, family and complete strangers. Emotions, intimacy, crying, caring, protecting, relationships, friendships, kindness, etc. are all from God, portrayed by Jesus and are necessary for being a healthy man.

Sometimes as a man we mix up intimacy with sexual attraction because the only intimacy we have been told about and know is sexual. Sex and intimacy are not the same thing and it is possible to have intimacy without having sex. You were created by God to have a need for intimacy which at its simplest state is a strong connection and familiarity within friendships. Sex is a deeper way to experience that connection and build trust with another person once a marital covenant has been established. We were made for intimacy with other men and women and having healthy male friendships, is very important. I would encourage you to seek out relationships with people who you feel safe with and can really know and love you. Most importantly seek out a deep intimate relationship with God and see what He has to say about you and who you are as a man.

If you are feeling attracted to other guys, it could be from being sexually abused when you were younger. If you know this happened to you, go and find someone you trust who can walk you through the healing you need. If you aren't sure if anything happened to you, as Jesus. He will lead you into all truth and let you know what has happened or what didn't happen.

There has also been a lie that we need to "experiment" with our sexuality and find out what works for us. The world says that it is okay to be curious with the opposite sex and test it out. This is not true. The enemy would love nothing more than to tell you lies like this, but God created sex to be between a man and a woman. This needs to become a reality in your life. Begin to hang out with healthy married couples and watch how they interact with one another.

Most importantly, be kind to yourself. We are all human and we all have things we are working through. Extend grace to yourself and allow yourself to process through this with the Lord. He is gracious and compassionate with us, allow Him to invade the deepest parts of your heart and invite Him into your mess. He wants to help you get free, and be all He created you to be!

Refer to these scriptures
1 Corinthians 6:9–11(NIV) Or do you not know that wrongdoers will not inherit the kingdom of God? Do not be deceived: Neither the sexually immoral nor idolaters nor adulterers nor men who have sex with men nor thieves nor the greedy nor drunkards nor slanderers nor swindlers will inherit the kingdom of God. And that is what some of you were. But you were washed, you were sanctified, you were justified in the name of the Lord Jesus Christ and by the Spirit of our God.

2 Corinthians 10:3–6 (NIV) For though we live in the world, we do not wage war as the world does. The weapons we fight with are not the weapons of the world. On the contrary, they have divine power to demolish strongholds. We demolish arguments and every pretension that sets itself up against the knowledge of God, and we take captive every thought to make it obedient to Christ. And we will be ready to punish every act of disobedience, once your obedience is complete.

Pornography

Q. *What is pornography?*

A. Pornography is any writings, pictures, films etc. designed to stimulate sexual excitement. Pornography is also anything from soft or adult porn, to material depicting graphic acts, live sex shows, advertisements, stores, music, novels, and more. Pornography has varying levels of perversion all of which are dangerous to engage in as they all have the same power to pervert God's plan for sex, intimacy and covenant.

Many pornography users struggle to distinguish between the pornographic "fantasy" and the reality of authentic, intimate sexual relations. Pornography often depicts sex without love and commitment and often pushes the limits of what is physically possible. Pornographic sex has no kissing, no cuddling and no real intimacy.

Q. *What does watching porn do to my mind, body and future?*

A. Viewing pornography has serious effects that will influence the way you think and act towards the opposite sex. It can distort the way you view reality and that includes the way you look and interact with women and men. It can damage friendships and lead to depression, fear, anxiety, shame and can create more issues than just pornography. Scientifically speaking pornography releases the same chemicals into your brain and gives you an almost identical experience as shooting heroin. Dopamine, the feel good chemical in your body is released many different ways from the food you eat to the exercise you perform. It's in these acts that release dopamine when we begin to get addicted to the feeling and desire more. In the context of pornography however, this feel good sensation released in your brain makes your brain want it more and more. It is this that begins to transform the way we think. Pornographic images and thoughts are stored not in your short term memory but your long term memory. Therefore it is very difficult to forget the images you have seen when viewing porn, and gives you a distorted view of sex. God is able to restore your mind and set you free from shame and this addiction. Seek for help in someone trustworthy that has authority in this area, find accountability, and ask the Lord to fulfill the areas in your heart in which you are lacking intimacy.

Refer to this scriptures
1 Corinthians 6:18 Flee from sexual immorality. All other sins a person commits are outside the body, but whoever sins sexually, sins against their own body.

James 4:7 (MSG) So let God work his will in you. Yell a loud no to the Devil and watch him scamper. Say a quiet yes to God and he'll be there in no time. Quit dabbling in sin. Purify your inner life. Quit playing the field. Hit bottom, and cry your eyes out. The fun and games are over. Get serious, really serious. Get down on your knees before the Master; it's the only way you'll get on your feet.

Dating/Relationships

Q. *How can I protect a girls/guys heart in a dating relationship when I struggle with pornography/masturbation/lust?*

A. If you are truly passionate about protecting the heart of the one you care about then I strongly encourage you to get healthy and work through those issues before dating. If you are already in a relationship I would find an adult or mentor that you can trust and work through it with them. This might look like asking for accountability, developing a purity plan and purity covenant, determining your needs, triggers etc. and making a plan that you can implement to begin protecting their heart again. It is also important to have an honest conversation with them and tell them your struggles and also what you are doing to change this and get healthy. If you are still single, follow those same suggestions and seek to get healthy so you can protect, love and honor to the fullest! Refer to the purity plan packet for more on this.

Q. *How can I meet my boyfriends/girlfriends physical needs in a way that won't cause them to lust?*

A. First of all you are not required to meet their physical needs in any way. In a healthy relationship, physical touch or quality time are there to show love and communicate your heart for the person. If they are only getting their needs met from you, it is not a healthy relationship. There are plenty of ways for you both to get your needs met in a healthy way outside and inside of your relationship. Having deep connections and friendships with other guys and girls will be helpful in getting needs met apart from each other. Staying connected to the Lord and being intimate with Him will help you both to get needs met and should be your priority. When your spiritual needs are getting met, your physical needs will calm down. Make sure you are both aware that you need to get needs met spiritually first, and then from there figure out how you can help each other not to try to get your physical needs met from one another.

Q. *My girlfriend/boyfriend and I are already going way too far sexually in our relationship. How do we get back on the right track and make a solid purity plan?*

A. First, I would suggest going and getting help from a trusted mentor. Someone who will be able to walk you through asking for forgiveness and breaking off any possible soul ties that might have formed. Then, if you still feel like this is a relationship worth fighting for, figure out what your turn-on's are. Write down things you know will stimulate you to make you want to go further with him/her and work on protecting those boundaries. The point of a purity plan is to help you get to the place where you can be with each other, have a relationship, and protect each other's hearts and purity. Think of it as your purity is a cliff. It is not about trying to get as close as possible and look over the edge of temptation, its about staying back 20 feet to make sure you don't slip and violate your heart or the heart of your significant other's. Although you have messed up in the past, you are able to be redeemed and free! I would encourage you to begin to bring Jesus into the middle of your relationship and allow Him to bring you closer together. Remember, you are dating a son or daughter of the King! Refer to the purity covenant and purity plan worksheet.

Q. *Is sexting or sending naked pictures wrong to do between a boyfriend and girlfriend? What if it makes them feel closer or more connected?*

A. To answer the first question, sexting is very common among teens and is becoming more common among adults. One of the problems with sending nude pictures of yourself is that you lose control of the picture the minute you send it. There have been several high profile cases of teens who have been humiliated when nude photos of them ended up on porn sites or sent around to many people in their school. Once you send that picture it can be posted and copied and sent to places you had no intention of sending it. Those photos can come back to haunt you many years later when you might be trying to get a job or apply for a scholarship. Also, in some states having underage photos is perceived as child pornography and you can be prosecuted. It is not a wise idea to send nude pictures of yourself on the internet or on cell phones.

Sexting or sending naked pictures between a boyfriend and girlfriend is not going to make them feel closer or more connected. It actually can do the opposite. It separates the person from their body and makes them just a body. If you are thinking that you feel more connected because of this, then you are confusing sexual behavior and intimacy. You want to get to know your girlfriend as a person and sending naked pictures or sexting will interfere with knowing who he/she is. Sexting separates the person and the soul, from the body and we are so much more than that!

Sexting only has one purpose, which is to sexually stimulate the people involved. It crosses a line of intimacy that should be for a husband and wife. So for many reasons, sexting or sending naked pictures between a boyfriend and girlfriend is not wise.

Q. *How do you tell someone about your past? When is it good timing?*

A. It is important to never let your intimacy level surpass your level of commitment. This means that if you have only been dating for a few weeks, it may not be a good idea to let the person in to your heart fully. I would challenge you to keep things from your past to a minimum and save the details for later down the road.

When you are telling someone about your past, it should be a celebration of how far you've come, not a "feel sorry for me" type of conversation. There is so much freedom and grace when you open up to someone you trust about your past. Talk to the Holy Spirit about when is a good time to open up to your boyfriend/ girlfriend. He will lead you into all truth.

Q. *How do I tell my parents (about my past?) (that I have been sexually abused?)*

A. I believe it is important for your parents to be involved in your life especially since they are in a place of authority over your life. They are there to protect you and guide you through your childhood as you grow up into an adult. However, if you do not feel safe with your parents then I would suggest finding an adult you do feel safe with whether it be a pastor, youth leader or spiritual father or mother, and talk to them about it. It can be as simple as just asking to speak with them privately and sharing what is on your mind. Remember that fear only has power over your life as long as you allow it to. You can do this!

Q. *Will I have a good marriage even though I have struggled with (porn, masturbation, sex, SSA, etc.?)*

A. Yes! Jesus has fully redeemed any sin imaginable when He died on the Cross, including sexual sins. That means that when you ask for forgiveness He sees you as a new creation and you should see yourself that way too! When your past is forgiven, it no longer has any influence to dictate your life, character or future. You are in control of your life, not sin! Refer to the purity plan and purity covenant packet for more on this!

Q. *How do I move on from past relationships?*

A. This feeling of being connected to a person that you've been in relationship with is called a soul tie. A soul tie is a fancy word for a chemical connection through sexual, emotional or physical bonding. The process for moving on is not to ignore these soul ties but rather let God restore, renew and transform your mind. This can all be done with a simple prayer asking God to break the soul ties that were made in the relationship. On the practical side of things, you need to collect everything from any past relationship you still feel connected to. It may be things such as pictures, clothing, letters, phone numbers, emails, text messages, and more. Anything that connects the two of you needs to be removed, deleted and thrown away.

Refer to this scripture

Philippians 4:8 My son, pay attention to what I say, turn your ear to my words. Do not let them out of your sight, keep them within your heart; for they are life to those who find them and health to one's whole body. Above all else, guard your heart, for everything you do flows from it.

Addiction

Q. *What is addiction?*

A. Addiction literally means to be "enslaved by" or "bound to". If there is anything currently in your life that you feel like takes precedence over your relationship with God or family/friends, it may be an addiction.

Addiction happens when way more dopamine than you actually require, is released repeatedly. This causes you to feel "bound to", and want more of something such as pornogrpahy, shopping, food etc.

Q. *How do I break my (porn, SSA, masturbation) addiction?*

A. The first thing you need to do to begin to break an addiction, is admit that you have one. Acknowledging that you have a problem and need help, is where your healing process starts. Next, it is important to tell someone you trust about this issue. It is so important to stay connected to the people around you who love you and care for you, and who can be there for you through this process.

Go back to when this addiction first started and figure out if something traumatic happened to you, or why this addiction began. This will help you to figure out the root of your problem.

Know when you are most vulnerable to this problem. Does it come up when you are all alone late at night, or when you hang out with specific people? When you can determine times you are more likely to fall into the addiction, you can set yourself up for success. Have somebody that you can call, or that can call you at these times that will keep you accountable.

Be kind to yourself! If you mess up, get back up and try again. Do not allow yourself to let quitting be an option. Keep fighting!

Refer to this scripture

1 Corinthians 9:26–27 (MSG) I don't know about you, but I'm running hard for the finish line. I'm giving it everything I've got. No sloppy living for me! I'm staying alert and in top condition. I'm not going to get caught napping, telling everyone else about it and then missing out myself.

THE FACTS

1 Cars & Contraception (60's)

In the 1950's, access to cars gave teenagers an independence unknown to the previous generation. When "the pill" came on the scene in 1960, women stopped requiring men to marry them before having sex because they no longer feared getting pregnant.

3 First US State Legalizes "No-Fault" Divorce (1970)

In 1970, Governor Ronald Reagan passed the "no-fault" divorce law in the state of California allowing marriages to be dissolved without providing proof that a breach in the marital contract had occurred. By 1985, all other states would follow. Currently, the US has an overall divorce rate of 50%. The US ranks 6th in the world for highest divorce rates.

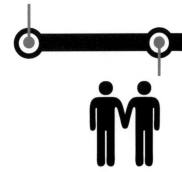

2 First US State Legalizes Sodomy (Homosexual Acts) (1962)

In 1962, Illinois became the first state to remove criminal penalties for consensual sodomy (homosexual acts) from their criminal code. Today, about 3.8% of Americans identify as gay, lesbian, bisexual, or transgender.

4 Supreme Court Legalizes Abortion (1973)

In 1973 abortion became legal in our nation. Since the 40th anniversary of Roe vs. Wade, the US has aborted over 54 million children. In 1995, Norma McCorvey (Roe) became a Christian. She is now pro-life. In 2005, she petitioned the Supreme Court to overturn Roe vs. Wade... her petition was denied.

REVOLUTION

5 STD's and Children Born Out of Wedlock (70's – Present)

Prior to the Sexual Revolution, there were two main STDs that people were concerned about contracting. Now, there are over 25. That's more than a 1,200% increase in 50 years. Today, 1 in 4 people are infected with an STD. In 1964, only 7% of children were born out of wedlock... today, 53% of children are born in the U.S. out of wedlock.

7 Sex Slavery (Today)

There are currently over 27 million people, in 161 countries, trapped in the sex slave industry around the globe. People are sold as slaves for $90 or less. 80% of these slaves are women. 17,500 people are trafficked into the US annually. Sex slavery is a 32 billion dollar industry worldwide.

6 Internet/Porn Industry (1995 – Present)

With the launch of the internet and with the increasing popularity of smartphones, porn has now become a 5 billion dollar world-wide industry. 7 out of 10 men and 5 out of 10 women view porn regularly. Sex is the #1 topic searched on the internet.

8 THE NEW SEX RADICAL

A PERSON RADICAL ENOUGH TO QUESTION EVERYTHING AROUND THEM & GET BACK TO GOD'S ORIGINAL INTENT & DESIGN FOR GENDER, SEXUALITY, MARRIAGE, & THE FAMILY.

FOR ALL SOURCES AND REFERENCE INFO, VISIT WWW.MORALREVOLUTION.COM/THEFACTS513

FOUNDER'S NOTE

Moral Revolution is an organization of radical lovers and passionate people. Like Dr. Martin Luther King, we have a dream of becoming a catalyst for a liberating global movement. We are committed to transforming how the world views sexuality, defines the unborn, embraces the family, and values all generations by honoring every human life.

We have dedicated ourselves to uncovering the root causes of moral decay that destroy the very fabric of our society. We have united under the banner of true love to help provide real solutions to these core issues and not just symptomatic cures.

It is our heart-felt conviction that a healthy culture is nurtured by positive reinforcement through intelligent and unbiased education. Honest, transparent discussion will achieve far more than fear, punishment, and rules.

WE BELIEVE THAT WHEN MOST PEOPLE ARE LOVED UNCONDITIONALLY, EQUIPPED PROPERLY, INFORMED EQUITABLY, AND EMPOWERED EQUALLY, THEY ARE PRONE TO BEHAVE NOBLY.

JOIN THE REVOLUTION, AND TOGETHER WE WILL MAKE HISTORY!

CHANGING GLOBAL MINDSETS BY
CHANGING CULTURE

FAMILY

CHURCH

CULTURE

EDUCATION

GOVERNMENT

START

LITTLE ME

LEARN IT

MORAL REVOLUTION
The Naked Truth About Sexual Purity

KRIS VALLOTTON
& JASON VALLOTTON

FOREWORD BY BILL JOHNSON

LOVE IT

WEBSITE

PODCAST

CONFERENCES

LIVE IT

40-DAY JOURNAL

LEAD IT

REVOLUTIONIST

LEADERSHIP CURRICULUM

LEADERSHIP WORKSHOPS

STAY CONNECTED

🖥 website

ⓕ facebook

🐦 twitter @MORALREVOLUTION

▶ youtube

podcast

➤ blog

@ email CONTACT@MORALREVOLUTION.COM

ADDITIONAL RESOURCES

MORAL REVOLUTION

This book takes a non-religious, gut-honest, fresh look at a subject as old as Adam and Eve. The wisdom within helps you and those you love emerge from the mire with your trophy of purity intact so you can present it to your lover on your honeymoon. While some nations seem to live in a perpetual orgy, and religion relegates the masses to sexual prison, people need to know they can overcome the power of peer pressure and push back the cesspool of distorted cultural values. You can take a Vow of Purity today—you will never regret the decision.

40-DAY JOURNAL

This Journal was created for you by people who are 100% passionate about seeing you experience health and freedom in every area of your life! Included are 40 daily topics to equip you to live with a greater understanding of how God created you, and His design for sexuality and relationships. This is a Smart-Book with embedded media throughout, furthering your interactivity and engagement beyond the written content.

REQUEST A SPEAKER

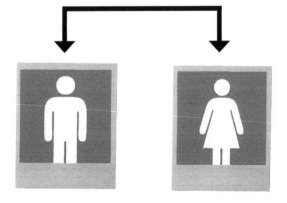

ADD AN ELEMENT

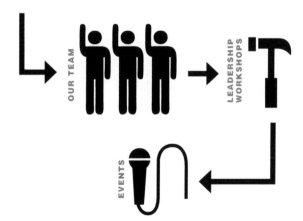

For more info, email: contact@moralrevolution.com

Join the MORAL REVOLUTION AND TOGETHER WE WILL MAKE HISTORY

NEWSLETTER PRAY DONATE